P9-CSE-923

Making Pet Palaces

Princely Homes & Furnishings to Pamper Your Pets

Making Pet Palaces

Princely Homes & Furnishings to Pamper Your Pets

Leslie Dierks

Illustrated by Orrin Lundgren

Sterling Publishing Co., Inc. New York

A Sterling/Lark Book

In memory of Tasha and Leo, two of the best cats ever known

Design and production: Charlie Covington
Photography: Evan Bracken
Illustrations: Orrin Lundgren

Library of Congress Cataloging-in-Publication Data
Dierks, Leslie.
      Making pet palaces : princely homes & furnishings to pamper
your pets / Leslie Dierks ; illustrated by Orrin Lundgren.
            p.   cm.
      "A Sterling/Lark Book."
      Includes index.
      ISBN 0-8069-8160-1
      1. Pets—Housing—Design and Construction.   2. Pet supplies.
3. Building—Amateurs' manuals.   4. Handicraft.   I. Title.
SF414.2.D54   1996
690'.89—dc20   96–18322
                                                      CIP

10 9 8 7 6 5 4 3 2 1

A Sterling/Lark Book

Published by Sterling Publishing Company, Inc.
387 Park Avenue South, New York, NY 10016

Created and produced by Altamont Press, Inc.
50 College Street, Asheville, NC 28801

© 1996, Altamont Press

Distributed in Canada by Sterling Publishing,
      c/o Canadian Manda Group, One Atlantic Avenue, Suite 105,
      Toronto, Ontario, Canada M6K 3E7
Distributed in Great Britain and Europe by Cassell PLC,
      Wellington House, 125 Strand, London, England WC2R 0BB
Distributed in Australia by Capricorn Link (Australia) Pty Ltd.,
      P.O. Box 6651, Baulkham Hills, Business Centre, NSW, Australia
      2153

Printed in Hong Kong

ISBN 0-8069-8160-1

Acknowledgments

Heartfelt thanks are extended to all who graciously allowed their animals to become photographic models for this book. These devoted pet owners include Maurice Antoni, Ivo Ballentine, Steve Becker, Amy Bracken, Evan Bracken, Jan Braun, Chris Bryant, Teresa Chalfant, Ailer Cook, Jim Cregg, Laura Dover, Richard Freudenberger, Charlie Green, Bonnie and David Hobbs, Dana Irwin, Susan Kinney, Sally Krahl, Shay and Jeff Kuykendall, Penny Leigh, Mardi Dover Letson, Celia Naranjo, Mary Parker, Jan Perry, Dorothy and E.J. Phillips, Ralph Schmitt, Brenda Sconyers, Mark Strom, Birch Terry, Pat Wald, and Cynthia and Brian Whitman. Thanks also to Ashley Maag and The Health Adventure in Asheville, North Carolina, for volunteer-ing their space and their guinea pigs, and to Jerry Heider at Superpetz in Asheville, North Carolina, for generously filling in with a few animal models that otherwise would have been sorely missed. Sincere thanks are expressed to all who assisted with the photography: Linda Constable at Sluder Furniture, Craig Culbertson and Otto Hauser at Stuf Antiques, Bonnie and David Hobbs, and Susan Roderick, all of Asheville, North Carolina; and Maureen and Lee Robinson at Dog Works in Zirconia, North Carolina.

Illustration: Dana Irwin

Contents

INTRODUCTION

The American Heritage dictionary defines the word *pet* as "an animal kept for amusement or companionship," but the more relevant definition of *pet* is the one that describes the word when used as an adjective: "especially cherished or indulged." If you examine the nature and extent of the pet industry today, it's clear that we're doing much more than just keeping our animals. We're coddling them with tasty treats, grooming them in fancy salons, showing them off in regional expositions, and even taking them to pet psychologists to unwind their emotional traumas. Pets play a major role in our lives, and the trend just keeps increasing.

Why are pets so important to us? As our lives become more complicated, more stressful, and more fragmented, the constancy and simple emotions of our pets offer welcome sanctuary. No matter how grumpy your boss was today, you can be certain that you'll be greeted with delight by your dog the moment you walk in the door. Your canary will sing beautifully to you even if you forget his birthday. Best of all, your pet stays with you during your bleakest of moods, when your best of (human) friends won't come near.

Pets have the endearing quality of enjoying our company. To most animals, we become a surrogate mate or parent when we adopt them, and they depend upon us to round out their social lives and provide them sufficient care and attention. It's well known that dogs are unquestioning in their devotion, but it's also true that animals as self possessed as snakes can suffer bouts of depression when deprived of their familiar

During a typical practice session, Malachite adds resonance to the bass chords.

human companions. The reputed indifference of cats is more than balanced by their desire to be right there with us whenever we're doing something interesting.

As the number of pet supply stores would imply, there is no shortage of accessories available on the market for pets today. However, creative people enjoy creative solutions to all their needs. In the pages that follow, you'll find 34 fun and interesting projects to make for your pets, including houses, play spaces, sleeping accommodations, and feeding stations.

There are projects for dogs, cats, reptiles, birds, and small mammals, and they range in style from whimsical to elegant, rustic to contemporary. Feel free to use any of these designs as a starting point, making whatever modifications you like to suit your own taste and needs.

A large number of these projects involve working with wood and using electric tools. Because this is a book devoted to pets and not to woodworking, a certain level of skill is assumed. Basic tools such as a hammer, screwdriver, and tape measure aren't listed each time because you will need them for nearly every project. If you've never countersunk a screw or cut a dado and the project you choose requires it, consult one of the many excellent texts available on basic woodworking before you begin.

One last thought to keep in mind: the fact that a project is shown in the cat chapter doesn't mean that your dog won't enjoy it. Whether it be a castle or a couch, select a project you like, and adjust it to fit your own "especially cherished or indulged" pet.

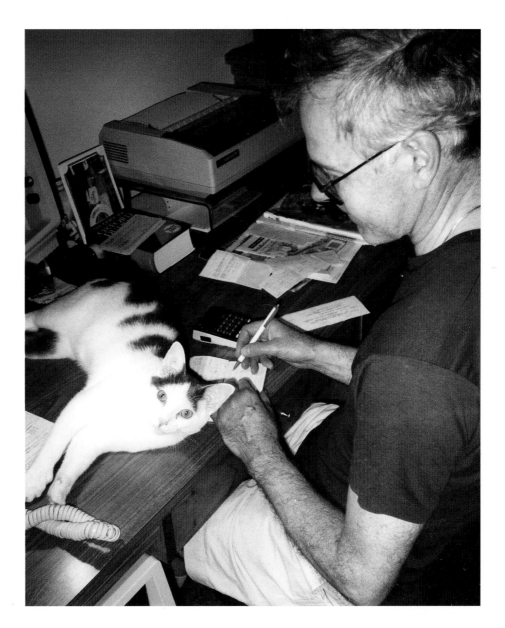

Mickey loves to help balance the checkbook.

Dogs

For more than a hundred centuries, dogs and humans have shared their lives in a relationship unlike that between any other two species. Dogs have willingly become guardians, hunters, and draft animals on behalf of their people and, in the process of doing so, have given something even more important—their loyalty. In return, we have lost our hearts to our dogs, often treating them as well as—or even better than—our children.

Part of our fascination with dogs derives from the fact that they vary so much according to breed. From tiny toys to giant mastiffs, dogs come in all sizes, body styles, and personalities. Regardless of what type of dog you choose, from an expensive pedigree with champion parents to a mongrel adopted from a local shelter, your pet will reward you with years of affection and companionship if you provide it a secure and caring home.

Canine Playground Equipment
Designs: Maureen & Lee Robinson

Agility training, as taught by Maureen Robinson, is equally fun for dogs and their owners. Working together, both get exercise, learn discipline, and generally enjoy each other's company. If you're serious about the sport, look up a trainer in your area; if not, give your dog and yourself an excuse to spend the afternoon running and playing. Cindy and her owner enjoy their turn at the tire jump.

Tire Jump

INSTRUCTIONS

◆ **1.** Prepare the tire for hanging by drilling three ½" holes through the middle of the tread, placing the holes at 3 o'clock, 9 o'clock, and 12 o'clock around the tire. Thread a ¼" hex nut, a ¼" washer, and the toggle portion of a ¼" toggle bolt onto each of the ¼" × 3" eyebolts. Install the hardware into the holes in the tire as shown in figure 1.

◆ **2.** Wrap the tire thoroughly in black duct tape. For contrast, add about five bands of white duct tape over the black.

◆ **3.** From the PVC pipe cut the following pieces: one 24" top, two 12" risers, two 36½" sides, one 39" bottom, four 22" legs, and two 2" connectors.

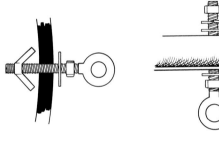

Figure 1   *Figure 2*

◆ **4.** Assemble the framework first *without* glue so that you can mark the joints and be certain of the alignment. Insert a 2" connector into the upward-facing opening of each tee and place the legs into the two T ends. With the Y portion of each sanitary tee facing down and the angled arm facing inward, attach the sanitary tees to the connectors. Then insert the 39" bottom piece into the angled openings. Put the 36½" side pieces into the remaining openings of the tees. Position an elbow on the end of each side so that the elbows face each other. Insert the 12" risers, followed by the last two elbows. Finally, place the 24" top piece. Adjust all the joints until they're completely square; then mark each connection with a pencil.

◆ **5.** Dismantle the framework in reverse order; then glue it together in the sequence just described. When using PVC glue, wear rubber gloves or take care not to get it on your hands; this type of adhesive is very difficult to remove from your skin.

◆ **6.** Drill a ⁵⁄₁₆" hole through the center of the top piece of the framework. Place a ¼" hex nut and ¼" washer onto a 4" eyebolt and insert the bolt upward through the hole so that the eye is facing down. Add another washer, lock washer, and nut (fig. 2).

SUGGESTED TOOLS

> Hacksaw
> Electric drill and standard bits
> Pliers

MATERIALS LIST

> 1½"-dia. × 24' PVC pipe
> (4) 1½" PVC 45° elbows
> (2) 1½" PVC tees
> (2) 1½" PVC sanitary tees
> (4) 1½" PVC caps
> 15" dia. tire

HARDWARE & SUPPLIES

> (3) ¼" × 3" eyebolts
> (3) ¼" toggle bolts
> (13) ¼" hex nuts
> (13) ¼" flat washers
> (2) rolls black duct tape
> (1) roll white duct tape
> PVC glue
> (5) ¼" × 4" eyebolts
> (5) ¼" lock washers
> 18" #3 machine chain
> ¼" × 1½" spring snap link
> (3) #12 × 1⅛" slightly closed S-hooks
> (3) ½" round-eye swivel trigger snaps
> (2) ¾" × 3⅛" × 10" utility springs
> 6½' #14 jack chain

7. Measure down about 1" from the lower end of each top elbow and drill a 5/16" hole. Install a 4" eyebolt into each hole as before. Directly below these eyebolts, drill two holes in the bottom of the frame and install the remaining two eyebolts. All of the eyebolts should be installed so that they are at maximum extension.

8. Attach the spring snap link to the end of the #3 machine chain and fasten it to the center eyebolt in the top of the frame. Open both ends of an S-hook and close one end into the round eye swivel end of a trigger snap. Then attach the trigger snap to the top eyebolt in the tire. With the machine chain dangling from the top of the frame, hold the tire so that the inside bottom is 30" (or lower; see step 9) above the ground. A second person is essential for this operation. Then insert the S-hook into the appropriate link of the chain. Detach the tire from the trigger snap and tighten the S-hook onto the chain.

9. The 30" height is standard for agility competition, but you can adjust this dimension to suit the size of your dog. For training purposes,

Maureen and Lee have attached additional trigger snaps along the length of their chain to obtain heights of 24" and 18". For very small dogs, you may need a height of 12" or even 6".

10. Install the remaining two trigger snaps onto the eyebolts at the bottom of the frame. Then tighten an S-hook into the round-eye swivel end of each trigger snap. With the tire hanging in place, attach the jack chain to one end of a spring and insert the other end of the spring into one of the eyebolts at the top of the frame. Pull the chain through the eyebolt on the side of the tire and attach the S-hook to the appropriate chain link at the bottom. Cut the chain, leaving a little extra length for adjustment, and repeat on the other side. Keeping the tire centered in the frame, adjust the jack chains so that there is some tension on the springs to keep them taut.

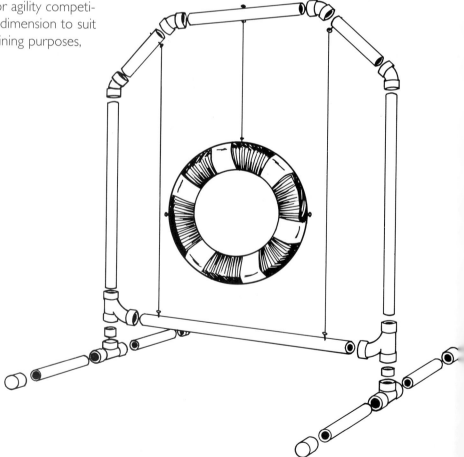

Bar Jump

Dogs naturally love to jump but are often put off by obstacles or something that looks like an unfamiliar dog. A bar jump will teach your pet to conquer those fears. These instructions tell you how to make a basic jump with simple plywood cutouts; vary the design slightly to substitute rectangular panels on the sides. In the photos, Saga masters the terrier jump, and Tribbles easily clears the panel jump.

INSTRUCTIONS

◇ **1.** From the 2 x 4s, cut two 30" pieces and two 20" pieces for the feet, and two 32" uprights.

◇ **2.** With both boards lying face up on your work surface, position one 20" piece and one 30" piece in a T, placing one end of the 20" board so that it touches the midpoint of the edge of the 30" board. Use a tee bracket and 1½" screws to connect the two boards; then further anchor them together by driving 3"

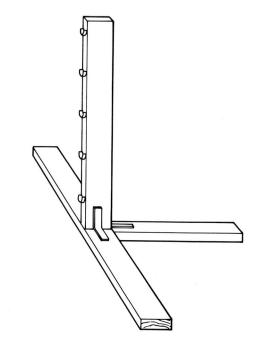

Figure 3

screws at an angle through the edges of the shorter board and into the longer one. Be sure to drill pilot holes before inserting all screws. Repeat this process to make a second T-shaped foot.

3. Turn over both feet; then attach a 32" upright at the center of each one, placing the edge of the upright flush with the top edge of the T (fig. 3). To connect the uprights to the feet, fasten three angle brackets or two 2 x 4 gussets on each assembly. (To make a gusset, measure 3½" down from the end of a 2 x 4 and draw a diagonal line connecting that point and the end of the 2 x 4. Cut along the line to make a right triangle 3½" on each side.) Use 1½" screws with the angle brackets or 2" screws with the gussets. Further reinforce the connection by driving 3" screws through the bottom of the feet and into the uprights.

4. One in every pair of closet bar holders is a semicircle. Use a hacksaw to cut the others into similarly shaped cups. Position the first cup on an upright so that when the PVC pipe is placed into the holder, the top of the pipe is 8" off the ground. Then attach the cup to the upright with 1½" screws. Place the second holder 4" above the first, so that the pipe will be 12" off the ground. Continue upward, placing cups at 6" intervals until the top position places the pipe 30" off the ground. Attach matching cups on the other upright.

5. Draw an outline of a dog about 18" x 24" on half of the plywood. Cut along the outline with a jigsaw and use the form to draw a second dog on the remaining plywood. After cutting the second silhouette, paint both dogs as desired.

6. Using the plywood dogs to determine the lengths needed, cut pieces of molding to attach to the feet and uprights to hold the cutouts in place. Position the molding to make slots that enable you to slide the dogs in and out of place as desired. Then attach the molding with 1½" finish nails.

◆ **7.** Paint the supports in the desired colors and wrap tape around the PVC pipe to make it more noticeable and colorful.

Alternative jumps with barricades: You can make simple panels by using readymade vinyl lattice work framed in 2 x 2s. Another option is to make barricades that are constructed like short sections of a picket fence.

Choosing the Right Dog

The typical life-span for a dog is from 10 to 15 years, and with improved diet and health care, it's becoming more common for dogs to live 20 years or longer. Since you're going to share such a lengthy period of time together, it's important to choose the right pet. Some major characteristics of the different breeds may be unfamiliar to you; if so, consult a veterinarian or your local library for more information.

Size is undoubtedly the single most important factor when selecting a dog. Although small dogs are often scorned as being poor imitations of the "real thing," large dogs are often relegated to an outdoor existence because they're deemed too inconvenient to be part of the household. If you view a wagging tail as a weapon of destruction among your cherished porcelains, consider the damage an 80-pound animal can do when he's excited by the sight of your neighbor's cat.

Running a close second in importance is personality. While some dogs are content to lounge in front of the fireplace, others are bundles of energy. Highly active animals need plenty of play time; those left alone much of the day are happiest if given a daily session of hard exercise. You must also be able to manage your dog's protective instinct, or the animal may become a liability. Dogs that are encouraged to attack may harm your best friend by mistake. If you want your pet to protect you against intruders, then invest in training for you and the dog.

When choosing a dog, don't ignore its grooming requirements. Long-haired dogs have greater needs than short-haired ones, and some breeds require professional grooming to remain healthy and attractive. Infrequent combing or brushing can result in a matted coat that invites fleas and ticks; if you try to comb through the mats, your dog may bite because he's in such pain. Although dogs don't sweat as we do, they do exude oil through their skin. Even short-haired dogs benefit from a daily combing, which distributes the oil onto the hair—improving its sheen—and minimizes doggy odor.

Holly, a blend of German shepherd, golden retriever, and Labrador retriever, is a giant when compared to Scully, a mix of beagle and chihuahua.

Kiln-Shaped Hut

Design: Penny Truitt

If you're a potter by profession, the natural shape that comes to mind when designing a dog house is a kiln, and your own handmade tiles make fitting decorations. For anyone else, this hut-shaped structure is remarkably efficient and easy to build. And the result is obviously quite comfortable to Heather O'Dell, a mixed-breed small dog.

INSTRUCTIONS

1. Make sure to measure your dog, especially his maximum width, before beginning this project. Then adjust the dimensions accordingly. The hut should be large enough to be comfortable, yet small enough to be cozy.

2. Cut two pieces of plywood, each 26" square, for the front and back panels. Draw a catenary curve by tracing the arc of a chain hung from each corner (fig. 1). Cut one piece with a jigsaw and use it as a pattern to cut the second.

3. In the front panel, draw and cut any shape for an opening that is large enough to accommodate your dog. The shape might be dictated by the decorative tiles you plan to use.

4. Cut a 26" x 22" piece of plywood for the floor.

5. Make a framework to provide a means for attaching the hardware cloth and front and back walls. Cut a 26" piece of 1 x 2 to fit across the back of the floor, attaching it on edge to the plywood so that there is a ⅝" gap between the 1 x 2 and the edge of the floor. This will accommodate the thickness of the back wall and allow it to sit on the floor. Then cut two pieces for the sides, each 18⅝" long, and two for the front, each 4" long. The front of the framework is inset 2" from the front edge of the floor. To fasten the framework to the floor, use 1½" screws applied through the bottom.

◆ **6.** Cut three additional lengths of 1 × 2, each 19⅜" long, to use as spacers.

◆ **7.** Paint the front, back, floor, framework, and spacers as desired.

◆ **8.** Using 1½" screws, fasten the front and back panels to the framework and attach the spacers at equidistant points around the curve.

◆ **9.** Place the hardware cloth on the hut so that it overextends the front and back walls by 2"; then staple the hardware cloth along the edges of the front and back.

◆ **10.** Paint the canvas with two coats of exterior paint. After it has dried, wrap the fabric over the hardware cloth and fold the excess under the wire mesh along the front and back edges. At the bottom ends, staple the canvas to the framework to secure it in place. Then add a final coat of paint.

◆ **11.** Using a tile adhesive suitable for plywood, apply the tiles to the front of the hut. Once the adhesive is completely dry, grout the joints. If desired, frame the decorative tiles with strips of lath or molding. These can be attached with waterproof construction adhesive.

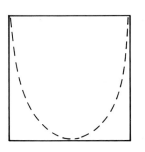

Figure 1

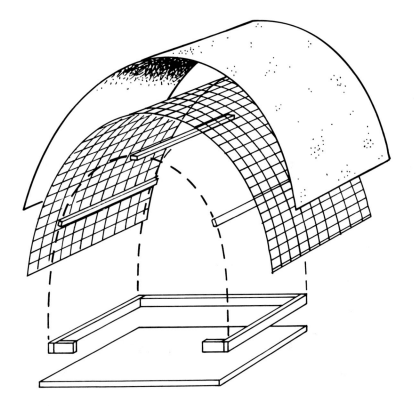

SUGGESTED TOOLS

Circular saw
Jigsaw
Electric drill and standard bits
Countersink bit
Wire cutters
Staple gun

MATERIALS LIST

⅝" × 4' × 8' plywood
(2) 1 × 2 × 8' pine
2' × 6' piece of ¼"-mesh hardware cloth
3' × 6' piece of heavy canvas

Short strips of wooden lath or molding (optional)

HARDWARE & SUPPLIES

Chain
#8 × 1½" galvanized screws
1/2" galvanized staples
Exterior-grade paint
Tiles
Multipurpose tile adhesive
Grout
Waterproof construction adhesive (optional)

Canine Café

Design: Norris Hall

Although she's no longer a young pup, Rosie considers herself a real hot dog when she drops in for a meal at her favorite neighborhood eatery. There she's guaranteed service with a smile from a courteous canine waiter who keeps a sharp eye on her bowl to make sure it stays filled.

INSTRUCTIONS

◇ **1.** From the ¾" plywood, cut two 7½" x 2¾" legs and the 8" x 16" bowl-holding section. Draw two 6" circles on the bowl-holding section, positioning them 1" from the front,

back, and sides and spacing them 2" apart (fig. 1). Then cut out the two holes with a jigsaw.

◇ **2.** Using a router or wood file, round the front and bottom edges of the two legs. Then round all of the edges of the bowl-holding section *except* the back edge. Make sure to include the edges of the holes. Using the same tool, round the front corners of the legs and bowl-holding section.

◇ **3.** Using an enlargement of figure 2, draw the outline of the back onto the ⅜" plywood. Then cut along the lines with a jigsaw.

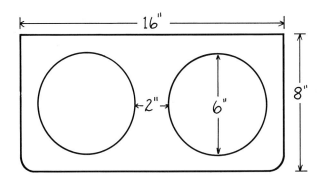

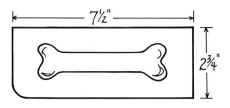

Figure 1

◆ **4.** Join the legs to the bowl-holding section with three 1 1/4" screws on each leg. After predrilling the holes, drive the screws through the bowl-holding section and into the top edges of the legs. Countersink the screws.

◆ **5.** Attach the back piece to the back edge of the bowl-holding section with predrilled and countersunk 1 1/4" screws.

◆ **6.** Fill all the holes with wood filler; then sand them smooth.

◆ **7.** Prime all the bare wood surfaces. Once the primer has dried, apply a coat of flat white paint.

◆ **8.** Using the photo and figure 2 as your guides, sketch in the design on the back. Paint all surfaces in the colors of your choice.

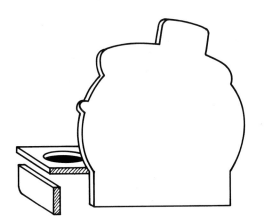

Figure 2

Kilmarnock Castle

Design: Mark Strom

Even if your dog's name isn't Prince, he'll love holding court in his very own castle. The structure is complete with crenelated walls and turrets, and a simple faux finish with stenciled block work gives it the look of ancient stone. Here Culley, a proud Scottish terrier, casts a watchful eye from the arched doorway.

INSTRUCTIONS

◇ **1.** Cut two pieces of plywood, each 23⅞" × 20". Find and mark the center on one 23⅞" edge of one piece. On the same edge, measure ¾" down from each corner and mark. Using a straightedge, draw a line from the center to each ¾" mark. This creates the roof slope, which is 5°. (In areas where heavy snow is common, the slope should be increased to avoid excessive buildup.) Repeat this process on the second piece of plywood. Then use a jigsaw to cut the marked lines.

◇ **2.** Choose one of the cut pieces for the front wall and draw a line down the center from the roof peak to the bottom edge. Measure and mark a point 13" up from the bottom along the center line. Then measure and mark 6" out from each side of the center line. Using a carpenter's square, draw the 12" × 13" door opening.

◇ **3.** To make an arched opening, set your compass to a 13" radius or use a piece of string with a pencil at one end and a push pin at the other. Set the point at the bottom center of the door and draw the arc so that the peak touches the top line of the door opening. Then cut the arched opening.

◇ **4.** Using the scrap cut from the doorway, draw and cut an arched trim piece 1" wide by 12" long (fig. 1). Use a 13" radius for the inside

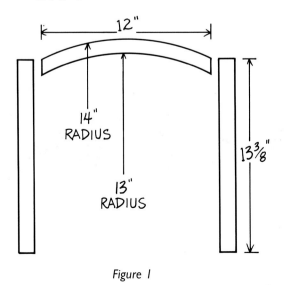

Figure 1

curve and a 14" radius for the outside edge. Then cut two rectangular strips of plywood, each 1" × 13⅜". Attach the trim around the doorway with ¾" finish nails and waterproof glue.

◇ **5.** For the floor, cut one piece of plywood 23⅞" × 36". Attach the front and back walls to the floor with countersunk screws, inserting the screws through the bottom of the floor and into the edges of the walls.

◇ **6.** Cut two side walls from plywood, each 34½" × 19⅜". One long edge of each wall should be cut with a 5° bevel to accommodate the slope of the roof. Using countersunk screws, attach the walls to the floor so that the lower edges of the bevels at the tops of the walls face into the box.

7. To make the turrets, cut the 4 x 4 into four 23¾" lengths. Attach one to each corner of the box using countersunk screws inserted through the inside corner of the box. Each turret should protrude 1¾" from the adjacent side wall (fig. 2).

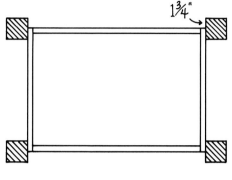

Figure 2

8. Cut two pieces of plywood for the roof, each 12" x 36", cutting each with a 5° bevel along one long edge. Attach the roof pieces to the box with 1" finish nails and waterproof glue, making sure to glue the center joint of the roof securely.

9. For the base trim, cut a 45° bevel along the full length of one 1 x 4 so that ¼" remains on the square edge (fig. 3). This trim goes entirely around the box and four turrets. Starting with the longest pieces first, measure and cut the pieces to length with a 45° miter on each end. All measurements and cuts are duplicated on the opposite side of the castle, so the pieces can be cut two or four at a time without having to measure every one individually. Attach the pieces using glue and countersunk 1" finish nails, predrilling for the nails to avoid splitting.

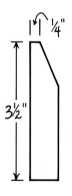

Figure 3

10. Cut a ¾" x ⅜" x 16' strip from the second 1 x 4. On each outside face of each turret, measure 6¼" down from the top and mark across. Repeating the process, measure and

mark 14" down from the top. Then cut the ⅜" strip into appropriate lengths to wrap each turret along the marks. Attach the trim so that the ⅜" dimension becomes the thickness and the ¾" side faces outward. Predrill each piece and attach it with glue and countersunk ¾" finish nails.

11. Rip a second ¾" x ⅜" x 16' strip to use for trim on the front, back, and sides of the castle. Cut lengths to fit and attach them with glue and finish nails, aligning them with the existing trim on the turrets.

12. For the crenelated top molding on the front and back walls, cut two pieces from the 1 x 3, each 20⅜" long. Along the top edge of one piece, measure down ¾" and mark a line across the length of the board. From one end of the line, measure in 2" and mark. Then measure over 1⅞" and mark; measure over 1¾" and mark. Continue alternating 1-⅞" and 1¾" marks until you reach the other end, where you will end with 2". Use a carpenter's square to continue the marks up to the top edge of the board. You should have five 1⅞" blocks and four 1¾" blocks. Using a jigsaw, cut out all the 1⅞" blocks (fig. 4). Repeat on the second board.

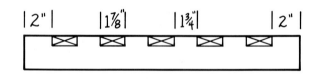

Figure 4

13. Make the crenelated molding for the sides using the same process. Cut two pieces, each 36", of 1 x 3 and mark a line across the boards at ¾" down from the top edge. Measure 2" in from each end and mark. From that point measure in at 1⅞" intervals until you reach the center. The center block should be 2". Using the jigsaw, remove every other 1⅞" block, starting with the first one after the 2" end block. Glue and nail the molding in place, making sure the bottom of each cut space is flush with the roof top.

14. Trim out the crenelated molding on each of the four walls of the castle by attaching a ⅜" × ¾" strip about three-quarters of the distance up from the bottom of the crenelated molding.

15. Cut the crenelated molding for the turrets in two steps. First cut a 45" length of 1 × 3 and measure and mark eight pieces, each 5" in length. Allow for the saw kerf between each piece. After drawing a line across the board at ¾" down from the top edge, measure and mark 1" intervals across each piece. Cut out the second block in from each end of each marked piece. Then cut the 45" board into 5" lengths as marked.

16. Second, cut a 30" length of 1 × 3 and measure eight pieces, each 3½" long, allowing for the saw kerfs. Measure down ¾"; then measure in 1" from each edge of each piece. Using a jigsaw, remove the 1½"-wide block in the center of each piece. Then cut the board into eight pieces.

17. Attach the 3½" pieces of crenelated molding on the opposite sides of each turret using glue and 1" finish nails. Position each piece so that the bottoms of the cutout areas are ⅜" above the top of the 4 × 4. Attach the 5" crenelated pieces on the remaining sides.

18. Countersink all nails and fill the holes and any open joints on the mitered corners around the base of the castle. Then sand with 150-grit sandpaper. Caulk all the roof joints and seams.

19. Prime and paint the castle as desired.

20. Raising the castle 2" off the ground is an option to keep moisture from permeating the bottom. Use 2 × 2 cedar or treated lumber, attaching it to the bottom with galvanized screws.

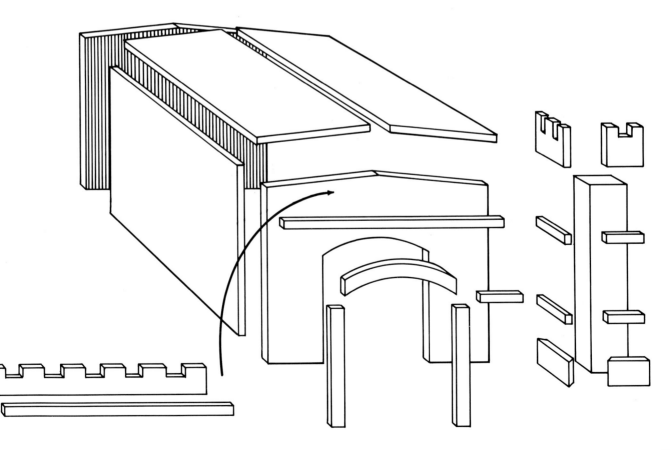

Fido's Rustic Hideaway

Design: Dan Mack

Dogs that live inside usually stake out a small table or bench for themselves, claiming it as a sanctuary to hide under when they're tired, scared, or ready to defend a stolen morsel or slipper. This rustic piece is modeled after the designer's piano bench and is equipped with several of his dog's favorite trophies. Trooper looks mighty pleased with himself as he guards his booty from his favorite spot under the bench.

INSTRUCTIONS

◇ **1.** Determine the dimensions for your hideaway bench based upon your dog and his habits. (This one works well for medium-sized dogs but wouldn't offer much comfort to a Pekinese or a Great Dane.) Then find and cut several straight branches or saplings that will fit your dimensions. If desired, look for interesting feet to put on the front legs. The two cow horns shown here were found at a flea market.

◇ **2.** Cut 11 branches to length to construct the framework. In this bench, the front legs are 18" (including the cow horns), the right rear leg is 18", and the left rear leg/post is 46" long.

Each of the four side rails is 27", and each front and back rail is 13" long. On the rear leg/post, leave the remains of a few side branches up near the top to act as hooks for your dog's leash and other belongings.

◆ **3.** If you have cow horns or similar bony structures to attach to the front legs, use wood glue to bond them to the branches. Other items made of metal or glass may require a different adhesive. After adding the feet, make sure both front legs are equal in length to the right rear leg.

◆ **4.** To make the front panel, measure down 1½" from the top end of each front leg and drill a ¾"-diameter hole about 1" deep. Then whittle a ¾" tenon on each end of the front rail. After applying wood glue to both holes and tenons, insert the tenons into the holes.

◆ **5.** The back panel has two supporting rails but is otherwise made the same way as the front panel. Measure and mark one point 1½" and a second point 9½" down from the top of the right rear leg. On the left rear leg/post, mark one point 29½" and a second point 37½" down from the top. Drill a ¾" hole at each mark. After whittling the ends of both back rails, glue the rails into the legs.

◆ **6.** Once both panels have dried thoroughly, mark the locations for the side rail connections. For the upper side rails, measure 2½" down from the tops of the three short legs and 30½" down from the top of the longer leg/post. For the lower side rails, measure 11" down from the tops of the short legs and 39" down from the top of the longer one. Drill ¾" holes at the marks as before, making sure the holes are on the inside-facing edges of all four legs. Whittle tenons on the ends of all four side rails, apply glue, and fit the side rails into the legs.

◆ **7.** Allow the glue to dry completely before attaching the seat. Many seat materials are suitable for rustic furniture, including branches, strapping, or rope. To make the Shaker woven seat shown, start by using an upholstery tack or staple to secure one end of the cloth tape to the underside of the left upper side rail

near the back corner. Bring the other end of the tape up and outside the upper back rail; then wrap it around and around across the front and back rails (fig. 1). When the seat area is covered, cut the tape and tack the end under the frame. This forms the "warp" of your woven seat.

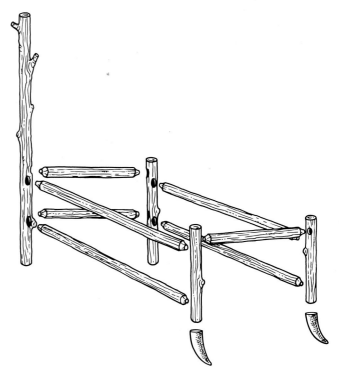

What's for Dinner?

Although dogs are carnivorous, they enjoy and require many foods in addition to meat. Meat is rich in protein, but it's low in fiber and some important vitamins and minerals. A certain amount of fat is required to maintain healthy skin and hair and to provide energy. Like long-distance runners, dogs also need a ready supply of carbohydrates to keep going.

Of the three most common types of commercial dog food, dry pellets or biscuits that are labeled "complete" are the most economical. (Those consisting mainly of cereal should be confined to snacks that supplement your pet's diet.) Canned food contains more moisture and generally looks more appetizing than the dry variety, but it's also more expensive. A third type of food is semimoist; it consists of meaty-looking chunks packaged in portion-sized plastic bags.

Some people like to share their favorite foods with their pets for special treats. Apart from chocolate, which is very harmful and can be toxic, most food groups provide some benefit to your dog. Fish, cheese, and yogurt are good sources of protein and minerals, and cheese is high in fat. Some dogs are intolerant of lactose, however, and may experience diarrhea or vomiting after eating milk products. Cereals and cooked rice are high-energy foods that also supply fiber and some important vitamins and minerals. Moderate amounts of fruits, vegetables, and nuts are beneficial as well.

◆ **8.** Part the warp slightly and tack the end of the "weft" to the underside of the upper back rail near the center. Working toward the left upper side rail, weave the tape under one and over one. Weave across the underside of the bench; then bring the tape up and over the side rail and weave the top surface the same way (fig. 2). Keep weaving across both top and bottom surfaces until the seat is full. Tack the end on the underside of one of the upper side rails.

◆ **9.** Decorate the frame with dog treats and your dog's favorite trophies. Add hooks for holding leashes and spare collars or for storing all those leather chews that usually find their way into the middle of the floor. To attach old bones and skulls, use drywall screws driven through predrilled holes.

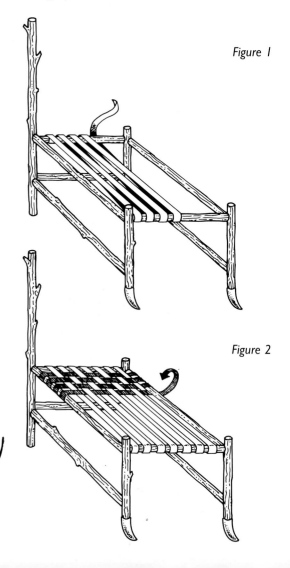

Figure 1

Figure 2

Dog's Best Friends

Design: Norris Hall

A hydrant, a bone, and a couple of canine buddies to yak with—what more could a dog ask for? This is a combination that's guaranteed to invite even the most blasé of pets. Sashi, who's a very cool cucumber of a Shih Tzu, takes special interest in the color-coordinated mattress with stenciled bone motifs.

SUGGESTED TOOLS

- Craft knife
- Jigsaw
- Router with roundover bit or wood file
- Electric drill and standard bits
- Countersink bit
- 1" paintbrush
- Artist's brushes
- Sewing machine

MATERIALS LIST

- ¾" x 3' x 4' luan or birch plywood
- 1 x 4 x 6' pine
- ¼" x 17" x 21½" luan or birch plywood
- Polyester fiberfill
- 2 yds. cotton fabric
- Matching thread

HARDWARE & SUPPLIES

- Poster board
- #6 x 1¼" screws
- #6 x ¾" screws
- Wood filler
- White wood primer
- White latex paint or gesso
- Assorted acrylic paints
- Clear acrylic polyurethane

INSTRUCTIONS

◇ **1.** Enlarge the shapes shown in figure 1 to their actual size and trace them onto the poster board. Then cut the shapes using a craft knife.

◇ **2.** Using the poster board cutouts as patterns, trace the designs onto the ¾" plywood. Make sure to draw two bones for the sides. Cut all of the shapes with a jigsaw.

◇ **3.** Using a router or wood file, round all the edges that will be exposed when the bed is assembled, but don't round any edges that will join other pieces. Sand all edges, especially those that will be visible.

◇ **4.** Cut three cross boards from the 1 x 4, each 17½" long (or equal in length to the width of your head and foot boards).

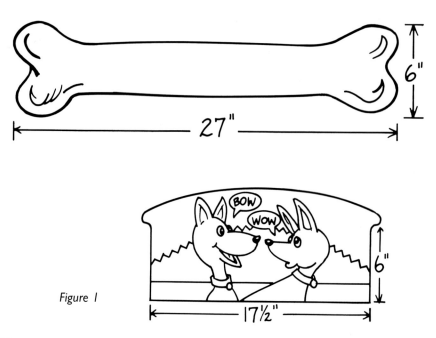

Figure 1

5. Prime all the plywood cutouts, the cross boards, and the ¼" plywood mattress board. Then apply a coat of white latex paint. Once the paint has dried, sketch the images onto the plywood with a pencil.

6. Join the side pieces to the head and foot boards with countersunk 1¼" screws. Make sure to drill pilot holes to avoid splitting the plywood. Attach the cross boards, evenly spacing them across the opening, by screwing them into the "bones" on the sides. Use wood filler to cover the screw tops; then sand the surface smooth when the filler is dry.

7. Once the bed has been assembled (except for the mattress board), paint the designs in the desired colors.

8. Attach the plywood mattress board to the cross boards using ¾" screws.

9. Apply at least three coats of polyurethane to the entire bed, letting it dry between coats.

10. Cut two pieces of fabric, each 21½" × 25", for the "mattress." With right sides together, sew them on three sides. Turn and stuff the mattress with fiberfill; then sew the fourth seam.

11. To make a pillow sham, measure the length and width of the finished mattress. Add a seam allowance to all four edges of the top piece. Cut the bottom piece the same width as the top piece, but make it 7" longer.

12. Cut the bottom piece in half widthwise and finish the cut edges with a narrow ½" hem. Overlap the hemmed edges by 6" and baste the halves together along the long edges.

13. With the right sides together, sew the top to the bottom piece on all four outer edges. Clip the corners and turn the sham right side out. If desired, add stenciled or painted motifs to the sham.

Pooch-Sized Adirondack Chair

Design: Patrick Doran

When the sun is bright and the afternoon long and lazy, everyone should have a comfortable chair and a good vantage point for surveying the surroundings, reading a good book, or just generally lounging around. Lucy, a Welsh corgi, likes to keep a sharp eye on her territory from her personal chair, which is about two-thirds the size of the one occupied by her human companion.

INSTRUCTIONS

◆ **1.** Rip the entire length of the 12' 1 × 4 to a width of 2½". Cut the ripped 12' board into seven 20" pieces, making five seat slats and the top and bottom back supports. For the middle back support, cut a 21½" length from the 8' board and rip it to a width of 2½".

◆ **2.** From the remaining full-width 1 × 4, cut three 20" pieces to use for the two front legs and front skirt of the chair.

◆ **3.** Cut two pieces, each 37" from one 1 × 6 to use for the back legs.

◆ **4.** For the arms, cut a 32" piece of the 1 × 6 and rip it to a width of 4½". Then saw the board in half diagonally, leaving a width of ¾" at the narrow end of each half-board.

◆ **5.** Rip the second 1 × 6 to a width of 3¾" to make the back slats. Cut one 24", two 23", and two 21" lengths.

◆ **6.** To begin the assembly, hold one front leg and one back leg together at the desired angle on the edge of your work surface. Arrange the pieces so that the top edge of the back leg intersects the front edge of the front leg at a height of about 14" from the bottom of the front leg. Hold the back leg close enough to the edge of the work surface to allow the rear part of the back leg to hang down about 1½" below the surface while the front leg remains on the work table. Using a pencil, mark the triangles at the front end and rear bottom

edge that must be cut off the back leg to make it flush with the front leg and rest flat on the ground. After cutting along these lines, check the fit with the front leg; then use this piece as a pattern to cut the other back leg.

◆ **7.** Attach the front skirt between the two front legs, placing the top edge of the front skirt 14" up from the bottom of the front legs. After predrilling the holes, apply 1½" screws through the front legs and into the ends of the skirt. Countersink the screws.

◆ **8.** Hold each back leg up against the back of the skirt and mark the angle cut necessary to allow the front seat slat to sit level on the top edges of the back legs. Cut both legs; then attach them to the back of the skirt, applying countersunk 1½" screws through the skirt and into the ends of the back legs. Use 1¼" screws to join the back legs to the front legs.

◆ **9.** If desired, bevel the top edges of the five seat slats with a plane. Fasten the seat slats to the top edges of the back legs, starting in the front and spacing the slats about ½" apart. Use two screws on each end of each slat.

◆ **10.** The back consists of five boards held together by three supports. Lay the five boards, with the longest in the middle, on your work surface. Space them apart evenly to give a total width of 20" and align the ends at the bottom. Using a straightedge, draw a line that joins the inside top corner

SUGGESTED TOOLS

Circular saw
Electric drill and standard bits
Countersink bit
Small plane
Straightedge

MATERIALS LIST

1 × 4 × 12' pine
1 × 4 × 8' pine
(2) 1 × 6 × 12' pine

HARDWARE & SUPPLIES

#8 × 1½" screws
#8 × 1¼" screws
#8 × 1¾" screws
Wood filler
Primer
Exterior-grade high gloss enamel paint

of one outermost board with the center top of the middle board (fig. 1). Repeat on the other side and cut along these lines.

◆ **11.** Place the top back support with its wide face flat against the back slats. The top edge of each end of the support should just touch the outside upper corners of the outermost back slats. Attach the support, driving two 1-¼" screws into each back slat.

◆ **12.** The bottom back support attaches on edge to the back slats. To make the connection, turn over the back assembly and use both remaining back supports, placed on edge on the work surface, to hold the back assembly flat. Position the bottom support so that it's flush with the bottom ends of the back slats. Then apply 1½" screws through the back slats into the edge of the bottom support. Remember to predrill and countersink the screws.

◆ **13.** Connect the assembly—without attaching the middle support—to the back legs by applying 1½" screws through the bottom

support and into the top edges of the back legs. Locate the front face of the back slats ¾" from the rearmost seat slat.

◆ **14.** The sawn edge of each arm will face outward from the chair. If desired, remove a small triangle of wood from the outside front corner of each arm to prevent the sharp corner from catching you in the leg whenever you walk by it.

◆ **15.** Hold each arm in position, aligning it in front with the inside face of the front leg, and mark where the arm meets the rear face of the outermost back slat. Attach the middle back support to the back slats at the marks, centering the support so that it overextends the back by about ¾" on each end. Join the arms to the supports with predrilled and countersunk 1½" screws. Finally, use 1½" screws to attach the arms to the top ends of the front legs.

◆ **16.** To add support to the arms, cut two triangular pieces from your wood scraps and attach one to the front leg under each arm.

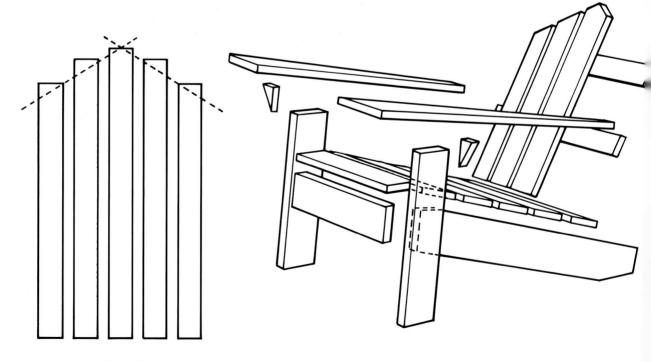

Figure 1

Doggie Yurt

Design: Blue Evening Star

Alternative lifestyles aren't just for people; Emma, a chocolate Labrador, enjoys taking shelter from the midday sun in her backyard yurt. Yurts are the traditional homes of nomadic Mongols, and they're well suited for situations wherever you'd like a portable shelter for your dog. If you put one in your backyard, it's bound to inspire some over-the-fence conversations with your neighbors.

INSTRUCTIONS

◈ **1.** Begin by making the lattice work that supports the structure. Cut 20 pieces of 1 × 2, each 24" long. In each lattice piece, drill three ⁵⁄₁₆" holes in the 1¾" face—one in the very center and one centered 2" in from each end.

◈ **2.** Bolt two boards together at the center hole and repeat with the other boards until they're all connected in pairs. With the bolt heads and top boards facing the same way, fasten two pairs together at top and bottom. This

completes one section of lattice. Repeat to make four additional sections, each containing four boards in a double-X configuration.

◈ **3.** Cut four pieces of 1 × 2, each 36" long, for the roof. At one end of each board, cut a small V-shaped notch. From the other end, measure and mark two points. The first is 4" and the second is 20" from the end. Center the marks across the 1¾" width of the board, and drill ⁵⁄₁₆" holes.

4. To make the door, cut four pieces of 1 x 2, each 20" long. Fasten the pieces together with glue and metal corner brackets, fastening the brackets on both sides at each corner with 1/2" screws. Position the brackets in such a way that there is room for you to drill a 5/16" hole at each corner.

5. At this point, it's helpful to assemble the framework and use it as a guide in fitting the canvas. Cut several short lengths of nylon cord and tie the sections of lattice together through the unbolted holes. Overlap the ends of the boards and orient the sections so that all of the inside boards face the same direction. Then tie the end pieces to the door. Open the lattice work into a roughly circular shape, matching the height of the door all around.

6. Tie the four roof rafters together with a piece of cord laced through the top holes. Gather the boards as tightly as possible into a circular formation. To stabilize the rafters, cut a piece of cord about 7' long. Lace the cord through the lower holes, but don't tie it together yet.

7. A taught cord around the top of the lattice-work supports the rafters. Tie one end of a long piece of cord to the top hole on one side of the door. Moving around the circle, place the cord in the gaps between each pair of lattice boards where they cross at the top. Pull the cord fairly tight and tie the end to the other side of the door. Then place the rafters on the cord, spacing them evenly around the circle, and tie the second rafter cord.

8. Using the circumference of the lattice work as a measure, cut a single piece of canvas for the wall. It should be about 12' long. Allow an extra inch or two at each end to fold under for a neat finish.

9. The width of the canvas should be cut to allow a 1/2" hem at the bottom and an extra 2" along the top. Across the top, fold under 1/2" and sew. Then fold under 1 1/2" and pin across. At 8" intervals down the full length of the canvas, sew a vertical line of stitching. This creates pockets along the top edge that can fit over the tops of the lattice work. Then hem the bottom edge and ends.

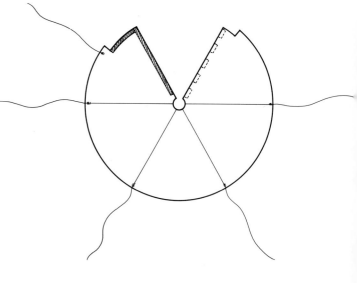

Figure 1

10. To make a pattern for the roof canvas, tape together several pieces of newspaper. Draw a 72"-diameter circle on the paper using a piece of string and pencil as a compass. In the center of the circle, draw a 4"-diameter circle and cut it out. Fold the large circle in half, then in thirds. Then cut a ⅙ section of the circle to use as your pattern.

11. Lay the pattern on the canvas and draw around it. Flip the pattern top to bottom and lay it next to your marks. Alternating top and bottom makes the most efficient use of your canvas. Mark and cut a total of five segments.

12. Pin the roof pieces together on all but one seam. Then check the canvas for fit by pulling it together into a cone and placing it on the rafters. The canvas should extend a little beyond the bottoms of the rafters to overhang the walls. After adjusting the seam allowances accordingly, sew the seams.

13. At the bottom of each seam, sew a 36" length of cord to use for tying down the roof. Then cut away the excess canvas that overhangs the doorway, leaving enough to attach to the top of the frame with hook-and-loop tape.

14. Sew strips of the hook portion of hook-and-loop tape to the roof canvas as indicated by the shaded areas in figure 1. Where indicated by dotted lines, sew pieces of the loop portion of the tape on the underside of the canvas.

15. On each end of the wall canvas, sew a strip of the hook portion of the tape. This will enable you to attach the canvas to the door.

16. Using a staple gun, attach strips of the loop portion of hook-and-loop tape to the top and sides of the door.

17. Fasten the tape on one end of the canvas to that on one side of the door. Working your way around the circle, maneuver the lattice work into the pockets along the top edge of the canvas.

18. Arrange the roof in place and secure the cords to the ground with tent pegs or branches.

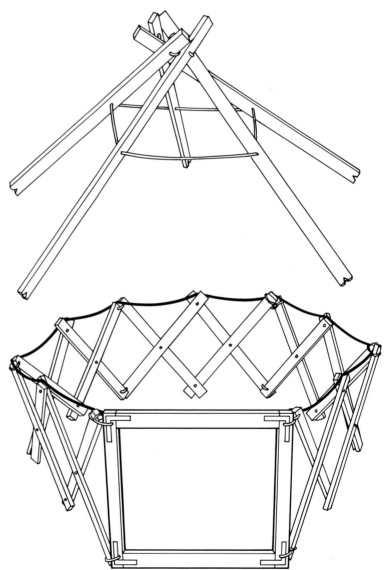

Woven Basket Bed

Design: Carla Filippelli

Honey, a mixed-breed pup, likes to survey her territory from the comfort of her cornucopia-inspired woven bed. The random-weave pattern combines round and flat reed to produce a rich textural harmony. As elegant as it is practical, this design fits any decor, from country French to Danish modern. Just vary the colors of the reed to complement your other furnishings.

INSTRUCTIONS

◇ **1.** Random weave is a very conceptual approach to basketry, with no set rules or patterns. As a result, it's generally recommended for those who are experienced basket makers.

◇ **2.** Soak your reed for 15 minutes in lukewarm water to make it pliable. Then use the round reed to make a coiled rim 24" across. Wrap the coil three to four times around, each time weaving it in and out of itself.

◇ **3.** With another piece of round reed, form the overall shape of the bed by looping the reed through the rim on one side and weaving up and down through the rim on the opposite side. Visualize a cornucopia as you work, but create a shape that's deeper and higher and not pointed on one end. This bed measures 29" deep and 19" high.

◆ **4.** To achieve the uneven shape, press down on the rim and slant it back toward the basket body. Press down sufficiently so that the bottom of the basket becomes somewhat flattened. This will help prevent the bed from wobbling as your pet steps into it.

◆ **5.** Weave the flat reed throughout the form, filling in the random spaces left by the round reed.

◆ **6.** Complete the basket by filling in smaller random spaces with round reed, checking periodically to make sure the basket sits well and has a pleasing shape. Attach the reeds to the rim every so often for stability. When you're finished weaving, tuck in or clip the loose ends.

◆ **7.** To make a cushion, measure the inside dimensions of your basket. Then cut two pieces of fabric to fit, adding about 4" all around to allow for ½" seam allowances and the fiberfill stuffing. With right sides together, sew the pieces together, leaving a hand-sized opening in the seam. Turn the fabric right side out and stuff the cushion with fiberfill. Then hand-stitch the open seam.

SUGGESTED TOOLS

Garden clippers
Sewing machine

MATERIALS LIST

3 lbs. 6-mm round rattan reed (#8)
2 lbs. ¾" flat rattan reed
2 yds. fabric
Thread
Polyester fiberfill

Old Dogs Can Learn New Tricks

Everyone loves a puppy—all full of wiggle and charm. He wins your heart, and you eagerly bring him home to share your life. Then, almost before you know it, his ungainly youthful habits have become memories, and his face now shows some gray whiskers. Is it time for him to retire to the hearth with an old slipper? Not on your life!

Dogs that lie around all day become bored, even depressed; those that remain active have happier, longer lives. As long as your vet agrees and your dog keeps up, there's no reason to give up that daily run together. When your pet begins to lag, just substitute some less strenuous activities. Instead of jogging two miles, take your friend for a stroll in the park or nearby woods.

With a bit of training, it's not difficult to teach an older dog to complete an agility course, track a scent, or master obedience skills. Dogs never give up their desire to please their owners and never lose their joy in being rewarded for a job well done. As long as they're given the opportunity to learn new tasks, most dogs remain young at heart.

If your dog's pace does slow as he ages, he can still remain active and alert by meeting new people. Take your dog along with you when you visit a friend or go to watch a neighborhood game of baseball or soccer. Although you'll always be the most important person in your pet's life, dogs are social creatures, and most enjoy the chance to make new friends.

Saga, a mature German shepherd, obviously enjoys her agility exercises.

Cats

Lovable but inscrutable, the cat has experienced nearly every type of relationship imaginable between man and animal. In ancient Egypt cats were worshipped as gods; in medieval Europe they were hunted almost to extinction. Today cats enjoy their rightful position as beloved pets and for the first time in centuries have surpassed dogs in popularity.

The independent nature of cats, which has earned them so much disdain from some, is the essence of their allure to many. Never fawning, always elegant, cats have their own timetable for showing love and affection to their owners. They won't necessarily greet you at the door or hop up in your lap upon invitation, but they'll thrill you in countless ways with their warm purr, engaging acrobatics, and gentle "kitty kisses."

Feline Fantasy Bed

Design: Norris Hall

Lola's dreams are certain to be sweet when she's surrounded by all these tempting fishes frolicking around the edges of her consciousness. Let your palette stray from the sensible colors of grocery store fish to those more likely to appear in the waters of your imagination.

INSTRUCTIONS

◇ 1. Enlarge the shapes shown in figure 1 to the sizes noted and trace them onto the poster board. Then cut the shapes using a craft knife.

◇ 2. Using the poster board cutouts as patterns, trace the designs onto the ¾" plywood. Cut all of the shapes with a jigsaw, making sure to cut two side pieces.

SUGGESTED TOOLS

Craft knife
Jigsaw
Router with roundover bit or
  wood file
Electric drill and standard bits
Countersink bit
1" paintbrush
Artist's brushes
Sewing machine

MATERIALS LIST

$\frac{3}{4}$" x 4' x 4' luan or birch plywood
$\frac{1}{4}$" x 17" x 25$\frac{1}{2}$" luan or birch plywood

1 x 4 x 6' pine
Polyester fiberfill
2 yds. cotton fabric
Matching thread

HARDWARE & SUPPLIES

Poster board
#6 x 1$\frac{1}{4}$" screws
#6 x $\frac{3}{4}$" screws
Wood filler
White wood primer
White latex paint or gesso
Assorted acrylic paints
Clear acrylic polyurethane

3. Using a router or wood file, round all the edges that will be exposed when the bed is assembled, but don't round any edges that will join other pieces. For example, on the head board, the side and bottom edges need not be routed. Sand all edges, especially those that were routed.

4. Cut three cross boards from the 1 x 4, each 17½" long.

5. Prime all the plywood cutouts, the cross boards, and the ¼" plywood mattress board. Then apply a coat of white latex paint. Once the paint has dried, sketch the images onto the plywood with a pencil.

6. Join the side pieces to the head and foot boards with countersunk 1¼" screws. To avoid splitting the plywood, make sure to drill pilot holes. Space the cross boards evenly across

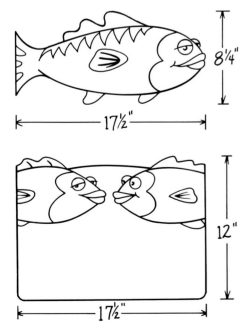

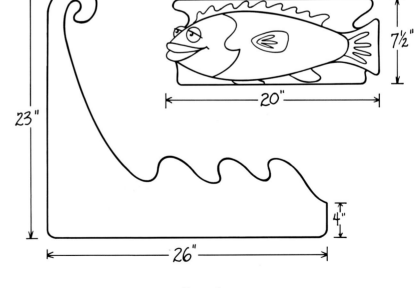

Figure 1

the opening and screw them into the waves on the sides. Use wood filler to cover the screw tops; then sand the surface smooth when the filler is dry.

◇ **7.** Once the bed has been assembled (except for the mattress board), paint the designs in the desired colors.

◇ **8.** Attach the plywood mattress board to the cross boards using ¾" screws.

◇ **9.** Apply at least three coats of polyurethane to the entire bed, letting it dry between coats.

◇ **10.** Cut two 21½" x 29" pieces of fabric for the "mattress." With right sides together, sew the pieces together on three sides. Turn and stuff the mattress with fiberfill; then sew the fourth seam.

◇ **11.** To make a pillow sham, measure the length and width of the finished mattress. Add a seam allowance to all four edges of the top piece. Cut the bottom piece the same width as the top piece, but make it 7" longer.

◇ **12.** Cut the bottom piece in half widthwise and finish the cut edges with a narrow ½" hem. Overlap the hemmed edges by 6" and baste the halves together along the long edges.

◇ **13.** With the right sides together, sew the top to the bottom piece on all four outer edges. Clip the corners and turn the sham right side out. If desired, painted motifs can be added to the sham.

Country Cottage

Design: Susan Kinney

Fred is an outdoor cat who likes to make his daily rounds of the neighborhood. At the end of a long prowl, he returns to his cozy cottage, where he can curl up for a well-deserved snooze. The style of the cottage is pure country, but it fits equally well into a city or suburban setting.

INSTRUCTIONS

◇ 1. Cut two 24" x 24" pieces of plywood for the front and back walls. To make the gables, find and mark the center point along the top edge of each piece. Measure down 7" from the top two corners, marking those points. Then draw a line from the center point to each mark and cut along the lines on both pieces.

SUGGESTED TOOLS

Circular saw or table saw
Jigsaw
Carpenter's square
Caulk gun

MATERIALS LIST

$\frac{1}{2}$" x 4' x 8' exterior-grade plywood
(3) 1 x 1 x 12' pine
10 sq. ft. asphalt roofing material
(2) 8" x 8" pieces of glass
Assortment of $\frac{1}{4}$"- to 1"- diameter branches
Sheet moss
Tree bark
An old brick
Dried flowers

HARDWARE & SUPPLIES

#8 x 1$\frac{1}{4}$" deck screws
#8 x 2" deck screws
Silicone caulk
1" roofing nails
Roofing cement

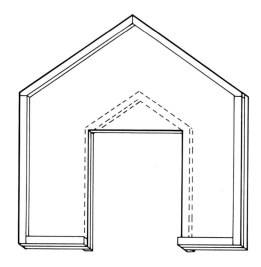

Figure 1

2. On the front wall, draw a rectangular door 10" wide and 12" high, centering the opening along the bottom edge of the front wall. Use a jigsaw to cut the opening.

3. Reinforce the front and back walls by attaching a framework as shown in figure 1. Cut four 16" lengths of 1 x 1 and join them to the side edges of both walls, placing the 1 x 1s flush with the edges of the plywood. Predrill the holes and drive 1$\frac{1}{4}$" screws through the plywood and into the 1 x 1s. For the bottom edge of the back wall, cut and attach one 22$\frac{1}{2}$" length of 1 x 1. Cut two 6$\frac{1}{4}$" pieces for the bottom edge of the front wall.

4. To cut the 1 x 1s for the gables, hold each piece in place and mark the angles on the ends. Then cut and join the 1 x 1s to the plywood as before.

5. After turning over the front wall (so that the framework faces down), cut four pieces of 1 x 1 to frame the doorway on the outside surface of the front wall. This framework will allow you to attach the vestibule. To match the roof gable over the doorway, find the center point at the top of the door and measure up 3$\frac{1}{2}$". This is the peak of the roof over the entryway.

6. Make the side walls by cutting two 24" x 16" pieces of plywood. Cut four 1 x 1s, each 21$\frac{1}{2}$" long, and connect them along the top and bottom of each wall, aligning the edges of the boards with the edges of the plywood. Both ends of each 1 x 1 should be inset from the shorter edges of the plywood by 1$\frac{1}{4}$" (fig. 2). Predrill all holes and use 1$\frac{1}{4}$" screws.

7. Cut a 25" x 24" piece of plywood for the floor.

8. Before assembling the house, test the fit of all four walls together with the floor. Attach one

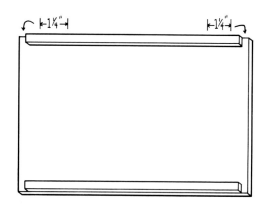

Figure 2

side wall to each 24" edge of the floor, making sure to place the 1 x 1 framework *inside* the house. Each wall sits on the floor, with its outside face flush with an edge of the floor. Join the walls to the floor by driving 1¼" screws through the plywood floor and into the 1 x 1 frames.

◆ **9.** Attach the front and back walls to the floor and side walls, predrilling all the holes and inserting the screws through the plywood and into the framework.

◆ **10.** For the vestibule, cut two walls, each 12" x 12", and a floor 12½" x 12". Cut four 11¼" pieces of 1 x 1 and connect them along the top and bottom of each wall (fig. 3). One end of each 1 x 1 is flush with the edge of the wall, and the other end is inset ¾".

◆ **11.** With the 1 x 1s facing into the vestibule, connect each vestibule wall to the house by driving screws through the plywood and into the framework attached to the outside of the house on either side of the doorway (fig. 4). Then join the vestibule floor to the walls.

◆ **12.** Cut a 21½" ridge pole from the 1 x 1 and bevel the top two edges at 30°. Then fasten the ridge pole to the peaks of the front and rear gables with 2" screws.

◆ **13.** To make the roof, cut two 16" x 28" pieces of plywood for the house and two 8" x 13" pieces for the vestibule. If desired, you can bevel the top (long) edges of each roof piece. This isn't necessary, since the seam will be covered by shingles. Attach the roof panels using 1¼" screws driven through the plywood and into the 1 x 1 framework. Center the roof panels on the house to give an even overhang.

◆ **14.** Using silicone caulk, seal all the seams of the walls, roof, and floor.

◆ **15.** Cut two starter courses of roof shingles ½" wider than the roof sheathing. Fasten this course, tabs up, to the fascia edge of each roof panel with 1" roofing nails. Cut and fasten the first true course of shingles, tabs down, over the starter course on each side. Continue on both sides with succeeding courses, overlapping by half, until the shingles meet at the ridge.

◆ **16.** To make cap shingles from the remaining material, cut the shingles roughly in half lengthwise, removing the portion of the material that has periodic cuts. Then cut the solid portion into appropriate lengths to match your shingle pattern. Use roofing nails

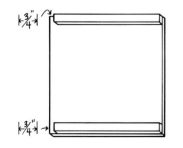

Figure 3

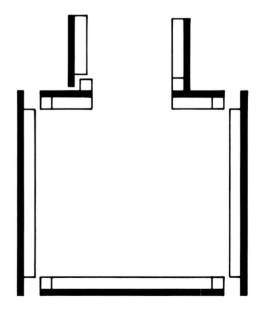

Figure 4

to fasten all the cap shingles but the last one over the ridge seam, overlapping them by about 2". The final cap must be glued with roofing cement.

◇ **17.** Cut two photographs of room interiors from a magazine and glue the photos to the two panes of glass so that each image is facing out through the glass. Using silicone caulk, attach the "windows" to the side walls of the house. Cover the edges of each pane of glass with a frame made of branches, attaching the branches to the house with caulk. If desired, create the effect of having a planter beneath each window by attaching bunches of dried flowers.

◇ **18.** Using silicone caulk as the adhesive, cover the sides of the house and vestibule with

pieces of tree bark. Sycamore bark is an especially good choice, since the tree naturally sheds large pieces of bark on a regular basis.

◇ **19.** Chip the end of an old brick to give it one slanted edge. Using plenty of caulk, place the brick on the roof so that it gives the impression of a chimney. Fill in around the brick with pieces of sheet moss, gluing them to the roof with silicone caulk.

◇ **20.** To complete the cottage, frame the opening of the vestibule with branches, attaching them to the walls with caulk.

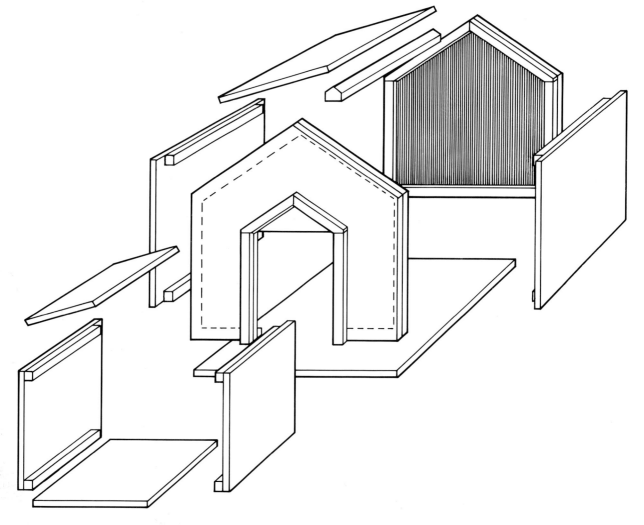

Indoor Cat or Outdoor Cat?

When you invite a kitten or cat into your life, you'll inevitably face the conflict between protecting your pet and allowing it freedom. The decision is easy when it comes to young kittens and valuable pedigree cats; keep them safe and sound indoors. But what about the six-month-old kitten/cat you recently adopted from the local shelter or the year-old tabby who's been begging you to let him go outside every day of his life?

Many cat owners in North America favor keeping their pets indoors to protect them from the dangers lurking just beyond the front door. This philosophy is strongly promoted by the American Humane Association, which states that indoor cats live longer, healthier lives than those who venture outside. Their literature emphasizes the potential dangers of outdoor life, including fleas, ticks, traffic, dogs, and other cats spoiling for a fight. There are other risks as well. Indoor cats, when lost, turn up in a closet or under a bed; outdoor cats can wander off or be stolen, never to be seen again.

Tasha rests near the wood pile, gathering energy for her next prowl.

In Europe the majority opinion seems run the other way. Their belief is that only pedigree cats and those in the process of breeding should be kept indoors. For other cats, a life of indoor confinement should be avoided if possible.

No matter how you feel about letting your cat go outdoors, it's abundantly clear what his attitude is. To a cat, outdoor air is an elixir, and the opportunity to chase butterflies is a gift from the gods. In short, it's pure heaven. His idea of a perfect schedule might be to begin the day with a romp in the grass, follow it with a hunt for rodents under the bird feeder, then to complete the morning, settle in for a long nap under a favorite bush. By then it's about time to go to the door, request entry, and beg a snack. What most cats really want is the best of both worlds—the warmth, security, and nourishment provided indoors, and the challenge, freedom, and excitement offered by the outside world.

Just back from the hunt, Leo strikes a regal pose.

To lessen the risks yet still give your cat the rewards of time outdoors, there are several things you can do. First and foremost, have your pet neutered or spayed; this will make any cat less inclined to stray or become engaged in battles with other felines. Before allowing him outside for the first time, keep the cat indoors for several months to become thoroughly familiar with and bonded to his home. Then establish the habit of calling your cat in for dinner and keeping him inside for the rest of the night. Cats are nocturnal creatures—as are many other animals—and are much likelier to get themselves into trouble after dark. Finally, if you're off at work most of the day and want to let your cat play outdoors while you're gone, provide him with some type of safe shelter or install a cat flap in your door.

Three-Legged Scratching Post
Design: Celia Naranjo

Lucky considers herself just that when she has her favorite scratching post all to herself for a lengthy session of claw grooming. With that complete, she usually likes to follow up with some stretching exercises to keep the muscles limber, then a few swats at the dangling rope, just to maintain her aim and speed.

INSTRUCTIONS

◆ **1.** Using a compass or a piece of string with a pencil at one end and a push pin at the other, draw two circles on the plywood, one 10" and the other 24" in diameter. Cut both circles with a jigsaw. Mark the center of the 10" circle and drill a ½" hole through the mark.

◆ **2.** Cut the cedar fence post into three 24" pieces. Then miter both ends at 30°, cutting the two mitered ends of each piece so that they're parallel to each other.

◆ **3.** Spacing the three posts an even distance apart on the 24" circular base, bring the top ends of the posts together to form a tripod. The 10" plywood circle should sit flat on top. Attach all three posts to the base and top using wood glue and 2½" drywall screws. Into each post, countersink two screws through the plywood top and two screws through the base. This is easier if you predrill all your holes and attach all three posts to the top before connecting them to the base.

◆ **4.** Starting in the center and spiraling outward, cover the top surface of the top circle with sisal rope. Use white glue and carpet tacks to keep the coil tight and hold it in place. Continue the coil so that the rope covers the edge of the plywood; then cut the rope and secure the end with tacks and glue. Repeat the process with the base, working your way around the posts as neatly as possible.

◆ **5.** After applying a liberal amount of white glue to one of the posts, start at the bottom and wrap the post with rope. Maintain tight coverage by frequently pushing down on the rope as you wrap upward. To secure the ends, use carpet tacks at the top and bottom. Repeat with the other two posts.

◆ **6.** Cut a 14" length of rope and push one end through the hole in the top circle. Make one knot at the top end of the rope to hold it in place and a second, larger knot at the bottom to entice your cat to play. If she needs further encouragement, rub a little catnip onto the sisal-covered posts and base.

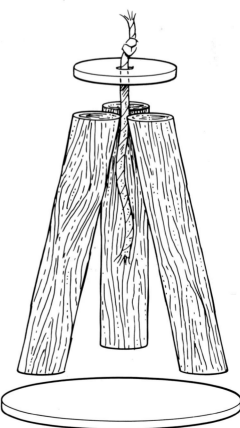

Cat Garden

Design: Susan Kinney

In the heart of every cat, no matter how domesticated, lurks the spirit of a hunter. The great outdoors is his jungle, where he can indulge every fantasy of the hunt and the capture. To create a garden for your cat is to set aside a corner of that jungle for pure pleasure and satisfaction. This one is designed for partial shade or sun.

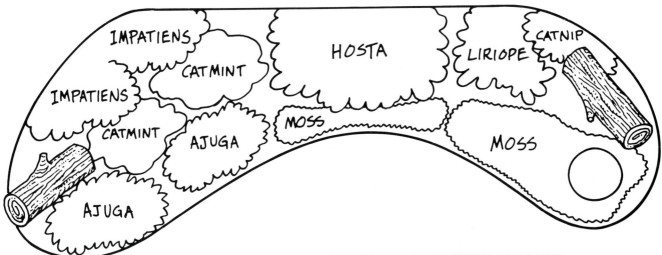

INSTRUCTIONS

◇ **1.** The area required is small, just 2½' × 8'. Use a spade to cut and lift out existing grass from the desired garden area. Then aerate the soil and add soil amendments such as manure and compost as needed.

◇ **2.** Position the plants according to the design shown here or as your landscape dictates, but keep in mind that each plant has a purpose. A large hosta provides shade for napping, and the moss planted beneath it makes a soft cushion and pillow. Catmint is a perfect plant in which to roll and get some exercise. Liriope or mondo grass is for nibbling, and catnip is your cat's equivalent of the local pub. Plan on replacing both of these regularly. For grooming the claws, include one or two logs. The ajuga and impatiens are there just for aesthetic purposes; use them wherever spots of color are desired.

◇ **3.** No garden would be complete without fresh water. For the fastidious feline, a few well-placed stepping stones are recommended to prevent the paws from getting soiled.

SUGGESTED TOOLS

| Spade
| Garden trowel

MATERIALS LIST

| Large variegated hosta
| (2) catmint *(Nepeta mussinii)* plants
| Large catnip *(Nepeta cataria)* plant
| (6) impatiens
| (2) logs
| Liriope or mondo grass
| Variegated ajuga
| Moss patches

HARDWARE & SUPPLIES

Small stepping stones
Small flat bowl or birdbath

Thai Palace

Design: Pat Scheible

For cats as elegant looking as Thai, a seal-point Himalayan, nothing short of a palace will do. This design suits her taste for beauty and her desire for a high vantage point. Its exotic styling belies its ease of construction, and the lightweight materials make it a breeze to relocate whenever your cat wants a change of scene.

INSTRUCTIONS

◇ **1.** Draw the four walls and base on the gatorboard. The front and back walls are 17½" wide at the bottom and 20" across at the widest point. At their peak, the front and back walls are 19½" high; they're 9" tall at the edges. The side walls are 13" x 9" rectangles, and the base is 17" x 13". Cut all of the pieces using a craft knife.

◇ **2.** In the front wall, draw and cut an opening about 8" x 8½".

◇ **3.** Using the walls and base as patterns, cut pieces of cotton print fabric, adding about 2" all around to fold over the edges. Sufficient overhang is especially important for the front and back walls, which overextend the side walls at the top edges.

◇ **4.** Attach the fabric to the walls and base using spray glue, pulling the fabric smooth and tight against the gatorboard. For the doorway, cut an opening in the fabric smaller than the hole in the gatorboard. Then make several short angled cuts and fold the fabric over the edges of the door, securing it with spray glue.

◇ **5.** Assemble the walls onto the base and join all the edges with epoxy cement.

◇ **6.** To make the roof, cut a piece of mat board 16½" x 34". Score the board down the center (making two halves, each measuring 16½" x 17"), but don't cut it all the way through. Then bend the board along the score line and shape it to fit the curves of the front and back walls.

◇ **7.** Because the roof overextends the house all around, you may want to attach fabric to the

underside as well as to the top surface of the mat board. Cut pieces of upholstery fabric to fit as desired and attach them with spray glue. Secure the roof to the walls with epoxy, positioning the roof with an even overhang all around.

◆ **8.** Complete the house by gluing fringe all along the edges of the roof and squeezing fabric paints in decorative motifs around the door.

◆ **9.** To make the legs, cover four thread cones with pieces of upholstery fabric and assemble each one by gluing a newsprint core on each end. (Industrial thread cones can be obtained from sewing outlets and custom drapery firms. Inquire at your local newspaper for newsprint cores.) Add a strip of fringe on each leg for decoration; then attach the legs to the underside of the base with epoxy.

◆ **10.** For the cushion, cut two 13" × 17" pieces of print fabric. With right sides together, sew a ½" seam all around except for a hand-sized opening on one side. Turn the piece right side out, insert the quilt batting, and hand-stitch the remaining seam.

Sultans of Sleep

Of all the mammals, none sleeps more hours of the day than the cat. Averaging 16 hours of sleep out of a possible 24, cats are expert nappers. Scientists haven't yet discovered why cats snooze so much, but they suspect that it's because the animals need to conserve their energy for the relatively brief but intense periods of activity associated with hunting and capturing their prey.

While your cat is sleeping, all of his senses remain on alert for danger. The slightest noise or nearby movement causes him to come fully awake, ready to flee. In fact, a cat's nervous system is so finely tuned that he can go from a tightly curled sleeping position to a fully extended leap within the blink of an eye.

Most of the time, cats engage in light sleep—the proverbial "cat nap"—and only about 30 percent of their slumber is what scientists classify as deep sleep. It is during periods of deep sleep that cats dream. Yes, dream. When your feline has his eyes clamped tightly shut in a sound sleep and his feet begin to jiggle and his whiskers twitch, he's in the midst of a dream. We'll never know for sure, but perhaps he's chasing a mouse or facing down the neighbor's tom.

Tasha enjoys her nap on the Sunday newspaper.

54

Window Seating

Design: Dana Irwin & Ralph Schmitt

Fergie loves nothing better than curling up on her very own bench to watch kitty TV (i.e., all the antics of the local birds and squirrels). Her favorite between-meal snack of mondo grass is right there at her claw tips, and the soft foam cushion offers a cozy place for a nap when the activity level dies down outside her window.

INSTRUCTIONS

◆ **1.** Cut the seat and sides of the bench from the 1 × 12 board, making the seat 5' long and the sides 3'.

◆ **2.** Using figure 1 as a guide, mark the curved cuts in the top and bottom of each side board. Use an 8"-diameter circle as a guide

Cut two 2 x 2s a little longer than needed for the angled pieces. Hold these in place and mark the angles on each end. Then make the cuts and attach the final pieces of the lattice.

◆ **6.** Fasten the lattice to the bench so that it's centered under the seat and the top rail touches the underside of the seat. Secure the lattice in place by countersinking 4" screws through the sides and into the rails.

◆ **7.** Construct two planter boxes from the 1 x 6, making each box 5½" x 5½" x 11¼". Miter the corners or make simple butt joints. Then cut the plywood bottom to fit inside the box so that it won't be visible from the outside. Use small screws or finish nails as desired to fasten the boxes together. For maximum versatility, don't attach the planters to the bench; they should stay in place once the cushion is fit between them.

for the cuts at the top; for the bottom use 4½" and 6" circles. A total of four circular cuts are required to make the pattern at the bottom.

◆ **3.** Measure down 10" from the top of each side board and mark a line across the board. Using a router or hammer and chisel, make a dado cut ¾" wide and ¼" deep on both boards at the line.

◆ **4.** Place the seat into the dadoes and attach it with 4" screws. Predrill the holes through the sides and into the ends of the seat and countersink the screws.

◆ **5.** Construct the lattice before attaching it to the bench. For the top and bottom rails, cut two 59½" pieces from 2 x 2s. Cut four 5½" verticals and attach these to the rails to create three 5½" square openings—one on each end and one in the middle. Fasten the verticals to the rails with countersunk 2½" screws.

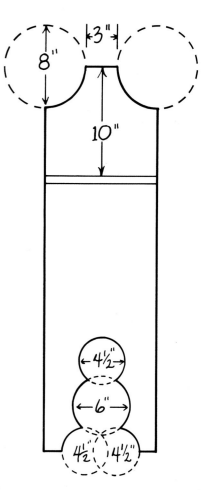

Figure 1

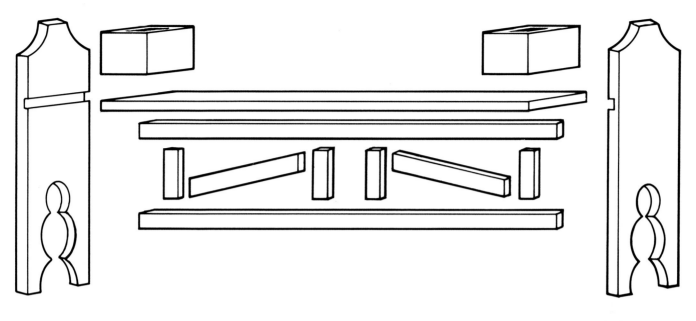

◆ **8.** To make the seat cushion, cut an 11¼" × 48" piece of plywood. Set the foam cushion onto the plywood, and wrap them both with upholstery fabric. This works easiest if you first set your fabric face down on your work surface. Then center the cushion on the fabric and place the plywood on top of the foam. Pull the excess fabric up onto the plywood and secure it with staples. Starting in the center of one long side, work your way outward, alternating one side, then the other. Treat the ends the same way you would when wrapping a package.

◆ **9.** Because of slight differences in measurement, you may decide that your seat cushion doesn't fit firmly enough between the planters. If so, use a few small pieces of self-adhesive hook-and-loop tape to hold it in place.

Claw-Resistant Garment Shields

Anyone who has ever shared home and hearth with a cat knows that a feline's favorite piece of furniture is some portion of her human companion's anatomy. Since cats tend to land and take off with claws fully deployed, unprotected flesh is likely to suffer. Mary Parker's cat Lydia favors her husband's shoulders, so Mary added "landing strips" on his pajamas. She applied fusible fleece to two scrap pieces of the same fabric used to make the pajamas, added contrasting piping around the edges, then top-stitched the shields in place on the shoulders.

Kitty Café

Design: Norris Hall

All the cool cats hang out at the local diner, where the food is good, and there's plenty of it to satisfy a hungry feline. After a long day of prowling the neighborhood, Balzac and Colette like to stop in for their favorite dinner of ocean fish and tuna in a delicate sauce. Slightly chilled fresh water tops off an excellent meal.

INSTRUCTIONS

◇ **1.** Cut two 6½" x 2½" legs and one 7" x 14" bowl-holding section from the ¾" plywood. Draw two 5" circles on the bowl-holding section, positioning them 1" from the front, back,

and sides and spacing them 2" apart (fig. 1). Then cut out the two holes with a jigsaw.

◇ **2.** Using a router or wood file, round the front and bottom edges of the two legs. Then round all of the edges of the bowl-holding section except the back edge. Make sure to include the edges of the holes. Using the same tool, round the front corners of the legs and bowl-holding section.

◇ **3.** Make an enlargement of figure 2 and use it to draw the outline of the back onto the ⅜" plywood. Then cut along the lines with a jigsaw.

◇ **4.** Join the legs to the bowl-holding section with

three 1¼" screws on each leg. After predrilling the holes, drive the screws through the bowl-holding section and into the top edges of the legs. Countersink the screws.

◆ **5.** Attach the back piece to the back edge of the bowl holding section with predrilled and countersunk 1¼" screws.

◆ **6.** Fill all the holes with wood filler; then sand them smooth.

◆ **7.** Prime all the bare wood surfaces. Once the primer has dried, apply a coat of flat white paint.

◆ **8.** Trace the design from figure 2 or sketch your own design onto the back. Using artist's brushes and the colors of your choice, paint the back. Paint the legs and bowl-holding section in contrasting colors.

SUGGESTED TOOLS

Jigsaw
Compass or string and pencil
Electric drill and standard bits
Countersink bit
Router with roundover bit or
    wood file
1" paintbrush
Artist's brushes

MATERIALS LIST

¾" x 7" x 20" plywood
⅜" x 17" x 16" birch or
    medium density overlay
    (MDO) plywood

HARDWARE & SUPPLIES

#6 x 1-1/4" screws
Wood filler
Sandpaper
Water-based wood primer
Flat white latex paint
Assorted acrylic paints

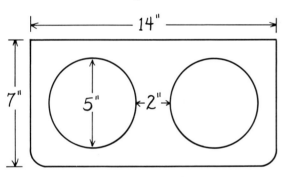

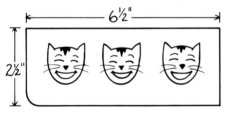

Figure 1

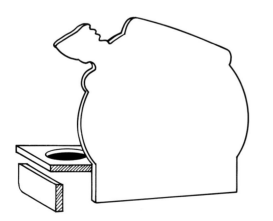

Figure 2

Upholstered Sofa

Design: Harold Anderson

Willie, a shaded silver Persian, has staked his claim on this cat-sized sofa. With its soft cushions and fur-coordinated upholstery, it will appeal to even the most finicky of felines. Since there's no wooden framework to build, it's any easy project to construct.

INSTRUCTIONS

FOAM BASE

◆ **1.** Using an electric knife, cut two bottom cushions 14" x 26", two arms 14" x 12", and one back rest 32" x 12" from the sheet of foam.

◆ **2.** Glue the two bottom cushions together to make a single cushion 6" thick. Do this by spraying a light, even coating of glue onto both pieces before pressing them together with your hands.

3. Similarly, attach the arms to the ends of the bottom cushion. Allow the glue to dry thoroughly.

4. Mark the back rest for the two cuts needed to allow it to fit between the arms and sit on the bottom cushion. This is easier if you first set the back rest on your work surface. Holding the sofa assembly perpendicular to the work surface, position the assembly so that the bottom of the back rest is even with the top edge of the bottom cushion. Then draw a mark along the top and inside edge of each arm. After cutting, check the fit and adjust if necessary.

5. To make the curve symmetrical across the top of the back rest, first trace the shape of the foam onto a piece of newspaper. Mark the center along the top edge; then draw a gentle curve down to the outside edge. Fold the paper in half and cut along the curve. Using this as a pattern, mark and cut your foam. Then glue the back rest in place.

SLIPCOVER

6. Use the same newspaper pattern as a guide for cutting the inside back and outside back pieces for the slipcover (see figure 1). When cutting the fabric, be sure to add ½" seam allowances on all edges. The outside back should include 2½" at the bottom to hem and fold under the bottom of the sofa.

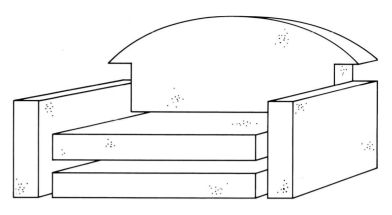

7. If desired, the arm front pieces can be cut with a curved top, as shown in figure 1; the other pieces are all rectangles. Cutting dimensions for all pieces are provided in the chart below, and the assembly arrangement is shown in figure 2.

Piece	Number of Pieces	Dimensions (width x height)
Seat	1	27" x 12½"
Bottom Panel*	1	27" x 9"
Inside Arm	2	12½" x 10"
Outside Arm*	2	15" x 15"
Arm Front*	2	4" x 15"
Inside Back	1	33" x 13"
Outside Back*	1	33" x 21"
Top Band	1	37" x 4"
Dust Cover	1	32" x 14"

Includes 2½" at bottom to turn under sofa

SUGGESTED TOOLS

Electric kitchen knife
Fabric measuring tape
Straightedge
Scissors
Sewing machine

MATERIALS LIST

64" x 32" x 3" foam rubber sheet
2 yds. upholstery fabric 54" wide
2 yds. elastic
½ yd. dust cover fabric

HARDWARE & SUPPLIES

Spray can of foam and fabric glue
Marking pen or soft pencil
Newspapers
Straight pins
Chalk

8. Using a ½" allowance on all seams, sew the front edge of the seat to the top edge of the bottom panel. Then sew the bottom of the inside back to the rear edge of the seat.

9. The inside arm pieces wrap up and over the arm cushions. Bending the fabric to follow the

angle cuts, sew the inside arm pieces to the inside back. Trim the seams and clip the curves; then sew the inside arms to the seat.

10. Sew the top band to the curved edge of the inside back and clip the curves.

11. To complete the arms, first sew the outside arms to the inside arms and top band. Then attach the arm fronts, clipping the curves and trimming the seams.

12. Before attaching the outside back, slip the cover onto the foam sofa and check the fit. Then, adjusting the seam allowances if necessary, sew the outside back in place.

13. An easy method for finishing the slipcover is to hem the bottom edge and sew elastic around the opening. For a tighter fit, place the unhemmed cover on the sofa and grasp the overlapping fabric in one corner. Cut out a V-shaped piece, leaving enough extra to make the seam, and sew a mitered corner. Repeat with the other corners; then hem and add elastic if desired.

14. Apply a scant amount of spray glue around the perimeter of the dust cover and the underside of the bottom cushion. Attach the dust cover to the foam; then fit the slipcover over the sofa.

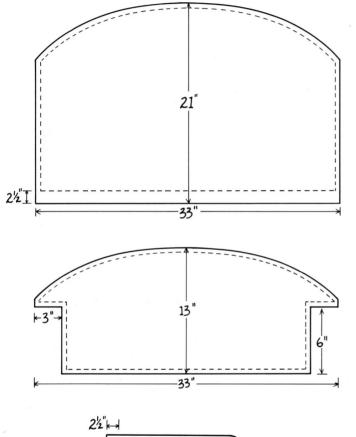

Figure 1

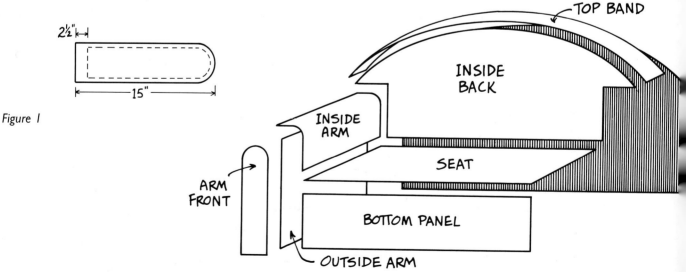

Figure 2

The Ups and Downs of Cat Fortunes

From Sacred Gods...

In ancient Egypt cats played an important role in daily life, first as hunters and pets charged with protecting valuable grain stores, then as sacred animals. Cats became the objects of worship due to the increasing popularity of Pasht within the pantheon of Egyptian gods. Pasht, the goddess of love and fertility, was depicted as a cat-headed woman and was sometimes accompanied by four kittens as attendants. Her temple at Bubastis was home to thousands of cats, all tenderly cared for by temple priests. At the peak of her cult around 950 BC, it is said that more than 700,000 pilgrims made the journey to Bubastis each spring for a great festival in her honor.

Egyptians so revered their cats that when a pet died, the entire family mourned. Dead cats were mummified, placed in cat-shaped coffins, and given elaborate funerals. Their bodies were given final rest in specially constructed cemeteries, where they could spend eternity in the company of thousands of other cats.

...to Handmaidens of Satan

As Christianity spread across medieval Europe, the Church sought to eradicate the stubborn remnants of pagan beliefs and customs. This had dire consequences for cats, who often enjoyed the company of herbal healers. When these harmless folk were declared witches by the priests, it was concluded that their pets must be agents of the Devil. A witch's cat was believed to be her "familiar," enabling her to cast her spells, and black cats were considered especially evil. During the 1400s, Pope Innocent VIII declared that when convicted witches were put to death, their cats were to be incinerated with them.

Throughout the Middle Ages cats were subject to torture and death due to superstition. It was believed that witches could take the form of cats, and strays were often killed out of fear they were witches in disguise. When plagues or other disasters occurred, cats were burned alive in an effort to halt Satan's evil work. One especially twisted belief held that good fortune would come to the occupants of a new building if a live cat were sealed within its walls or under the floor during construction.

Rustic Cat Tree

Design: Don Osby

Trees and large shrubs are magnets for
cats, who love to run full tilt up the
trunks and nestle themselves among the
branches, where they can keep a lookout
for birds or other cats. You can make
your cat a safer alternative using a large
woody shrub, such as a rhododendron or
mountain laurel, or a few young saplings.
Colette demonstrates how enjoyable the
finished project can be.

INSTRUCTIONS

◇ **1.** Using cord as a temporary binding, arrange two or three main branches to create a balanced form. As you try various shapes, make sure there are enough contact points where branches can be screwed together. Also look for two locations where you could attach two platforms. Platform areas should have at least three small branches for each to provide balanced support, and they should be located on opposite sides of the tree to prevent tipping.

◇ **2.** Once you've established the overall form, predrill the contact points and join the branches with countersunk #8 galvanized screws. The screws should be long enough to establish a firm connection without completely penetrating the second branch.

◇ **3.** Using a level or a plumb bob, orient the main branches of the tree so that they're perpendicular to the floor. Then make a mark an inch or so above the floor around the circumference of the branch grouping. Carefully cut along the line with a crosscut saw to create a flat and level surface.

◇ **4.** To make the base and platforms, draw a 22" circle and two 10" x 15" ovals on the plywood; then cut the shapes with a jigsaw. Cover the exposed edges of the three plywood pieces by wrapping them with grapevine. As you bend the vine around the edges, secure it with wire brads as needed to hold it in place.

◇ **5.** Place the branches in the center of the base and drill through the bottom with a countersink bit. Then join the base and tree with three 3" screws.

SUGGESTED TOOLS

Pruning saw
Electric drill and standard bits
Countersink bit
Level
Crosscut saw
Jigsaw

MATERIALS LIST

2 or 3 twisted saplings or
    laurel branches
$5/8$" x 4' x 4' plywood
30' to 40' of grapevine

HARDWARE & SUPPLIES

Cord or thin rope
#8 x $2\frac{1}{2}$" galvanized screws
#8 x 3" galvanized screws
#8 x $1\frac{1}{4}$" galvanized screws
$3/4$" wire brads
Polyurethane (optional)

◇ **6.** With the tree standing upright on the floor, use a level to mark the support branches for the two platforms. Then use a crosscut saw held parallel to the floor to trim the branches along the marks.

◇ **7.** Place each platform onto its support branches and drill countersunk pilot holes through the platform top and into each branch. Fasten the platforms to the branches with $1\frac{1}{4}$" screws.

◇ **8.** If desired, a coat of polyurethane may be applied to the tree, platforms, and base.

Reptiles

Two hundred million years ago, when dinosaurs walked the earth, reptiles were kings. They've never quite matched that status since, but the interest in reptiles is rapidly expanding in all sectors of the population, especially among children.

There are nearly 6,000 species of reptiles, including lizards, snakes, turtles, members of the crocodile family, and the tuatara. They all share certain characteristics such as scaly skin and a body temperature that depends upon their immediate environment, and they come in an amazing array of shapes, sizes, and colors.

Reptiles are among of the least demanding of pets. Their requirements for food and shelter are very basic, and they don't disrupt your household with constant noise or demands for attention. In return, they're fascinating to observe and handle. More than any other type of pet, reptiles provide a direct link to the uncivilized natural world; they're a window to the distant past when they, not we, ruled the world.

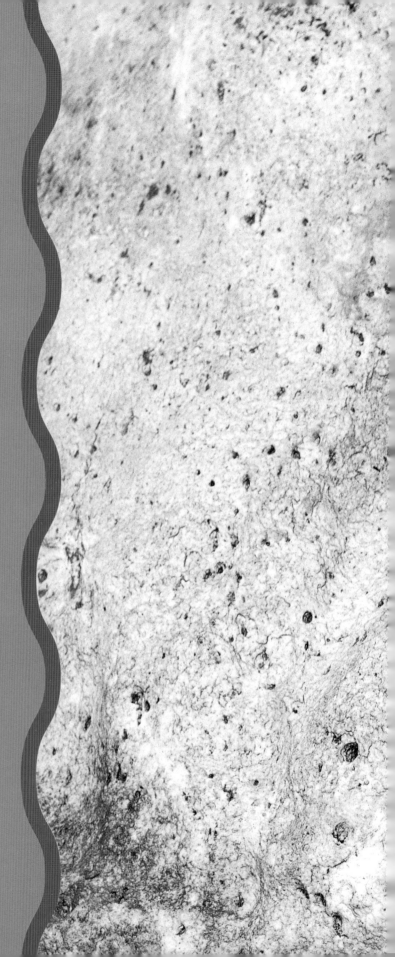

Reptilian TV Habitat

Design: Jeff Kuykendall

Why park yourself in front of the boob tube to watch old reruns when you can tune in and turn on to your reptile friends instead? Asia, a Chinese water dragon, effortlessly demonstrates that she makes a much better lounge lizard than any late-night TV host. Recycling an old television console not only provides a splendid home for your pet, but it also helps the environment. The added plus is that very little construction is required.

INSTRUCTIONS

◈ **1.** Flea markets and TV repair shops are great sources for old console television sets that can't be fixed, and you may be able to find a cabinet that has already been gutted.

◈ **2.** If you're working with a complete TV, start by removing the back panel. (Caution: Make certain the TV is *not* plugged in before you start.) The number of parts that must be removed may look intimidating, but the work isn't difficult. To help save time, use a ¼" socket in your electric drill to remove the screws holding the parts in place. Remove one component at a time, clipping any connecting wires. Take your time and remove everything else before handling the picture tube.

◈ **3.** Be especially careful when removing the picture tube. Picture tubes are both extremely fragile and quite heavy; in addition, they can be very hazardous if broken. Another pair of hands is recommended for this step. First determine if the tube will exit the cabinet through the front or the back; then position yourself and your helper accordingly. Remove

SUGGESTED TOOLS

Reversible electric drill
$1/4$" socket with adapter to fit drill
Wire cutters
Circular saw
Nailset
Staple gun

MATERIALS LIST

Old console TV
24" fluorescent light fixture with
  cover
Self-adhesive linoleum tiles
$1/2$" quarter-round molding
$1/2$" plywood to fit back of console
9" x 11" piece of $1/4$"-mesh
  hardware cloth

$1/2$" flat molding
$1/4$" acrylic sheet cut to fit front
  of console

HARDWARE & SUPPLIES

$11/4$" finish nails
Wood filler
Insulated staples
$3/8$" staples
Brads or small finish nails
Stain
Polyurethane
(2) 2" hinges
(2) eye-hooks
(4) casters

---

the screws from the sides and bottom of the tube, keeping one in place at the top. Holding the picture tube from below, remove the final screw and pull the tube from the console.

4. Use a damp cloth to wipe off any dust and dirt from the interior walls and floor of the console. To make a smooth surface that's easy to clean, apply self-adhesive tiles to the floor. Cover the walls with tile as well if the wood inside the cabinet feels rough.

5. Cut pieces of quarter-round molding to finish all the corner seams of the tile, applying the molding with $11/4$" finish nails. Countersink the nails and fill the holes.

6. Mount the acrylic sheet on the front of the console. The design of the cabinet will dictate whether to fasten the acrylic sheet to the wood with screws or use strips of quarter-round molding to hold it in place.

7. Install the fluorescent light fixture on the ceiling inside the console. Using a hammer and insulated staples, neatly tack the wire out through one corner of the back opening.

8. Cut a plywood door to cover the entire back of the cabinet, adding ventilation for your pet

by cutting a rectangular hole 8" x 10" in the upper central portion of the door. Make a notch in one corner, if necessary, to accommodate the wire from the fluorescent light just installed.

9. Cover the hole in the door with a 9" x 11" piece of hardware cloth, using $3/8$" staples to hold the mesh in place. Cover the edges of the wire with strips of $1/2$" flat molding cut to fit. To attach the molding, use brads or small finish nails.

10. Stain or otherwise finish the door to match the rest of the cabinet. When the stain is dry, apply two or more coats of polyurethane.

11. Mount the hinges on the console and door. Then attach two eye-hooks, making sure the hooks hold the door securely closed.

12. Attach casters to the bottom of the cabinet to make it easy to move and clean.

13. Before bringing your pets into their new home, allow any fumes to dissipate completely.

Cozy Snake Bungalow

Design: Brian Whitman

Small snakes such as Buka, a miniature boa constrictor, are less demanding than their larger cousins when it comes to real estate. With an expected maximum size of $3\frac{1}{2}$ feet and weight of about three pounds, it's unlikely Buka will ever outgrow this snug wooden lodge. It measures just 25" by $12\frac{1}{2}$" by 18" and fits easily into any room of your own home.

INSTRUCTIONS

◆ **1.** From the $\frac{1}{2}$" plywood, cut two $11\frac{1}{2}$" × 24" pieces for the top and bottom. Use a jigsaw to cut a $9\frac{1}{4}$" square opening in the center of the top piece.

◆ **2.** Cut two pieces of plywood, one $16\frac{3}{4}$" × 18" and the other $7\frac{1}{4}$" × 18", for the front. In the larger piece (the door), cut a $12\frac{3}{4}$" × 15" rectangular opening, placing it 2½" from the left edge and 1½" from the top, bottom, and right edges. Cut a 4¼" × 15" rectangular opening in the smaller piece (the window), placing the opening 1½" from each edge.

◆ **3.** For the sides, cut two pieces of plywood, each 12½" × 18". Then cut four 17" and four 4½" support pieces from the 1 × 4. Using 1" finish nails, attach two long and two short 1 × 4 supports to each plywood side as shown in figure 1. Inset the boards ½" from the edges of the plywood.

◆ **4.** Drill several vent holes near the bottom through both side pieces. Gauge the size of the holes based upon the size of your snake; the purpose of the holes is to allow gases from fecal matter to escape, not to permit your snake to wander around the house uninvited.

◆ **5.** Cut a 24" × 18" piece of plywood for the back.

◆ **6.** Before assembling the structure, stain all the pieces. Once the stain is dry, apply one or two coats of polyurethane to the outside surfaces and three or four coats to the inside.

◆ **7.** Attach the square piece of hardware cloth to the inside surface of the top piece, covering the hole evenly. Stretch the wire so that it's

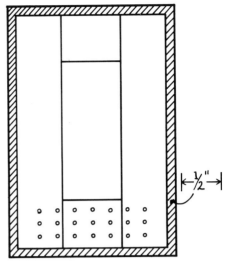

Figure 1

tight; then secure it with ⅜" screws or staples at many points to avoid unplanned escapes later. If you use screws, predrill slightly smaller pilot holes.

◆ **8.** To install the acrylic sheets in the door and window, first predrill holes through the plastic just large enough to accept the ½" round-head screws. When connecting the acrylic sheets to the plywood, make sure to get a good flat seal between the two to help maintain climate control for the future inhabitant.

SUGGESTED TOOLS

Circular saw
Jigsaw
Electric drill and standard bits
Carpenter's square
Tape measure

MATERIALS LIST

½" × 4' × 5' plywood
1 × 4 × 12'
1 × 2 × 17"
¼" × 13¾" × 16" acrylic sheet
¼" × 5¼" × 16" acrylic sheet
12" square piece of ¼"-mesh
    hardware cloth

HARDWARE & SUPPLIES

1" finish nails
⅜" screws or staples
½" round-head screws
1¼" finish nails
(2) 2" hinges
Door handle
(2) 1½" eye-hooks
(6) rubber feet
Weather stripping
Stain
Satin polyurethane
Clear silicone caulk

9. Begin assembling the cabinet by joining the sides to the bottom, driving 1¼" nails through the bottom plywood and into the edges of the 1 x 4 supports on the side walls. Then nail the back to the sides and bottom. When joining the back to the bottom, it may be helpful to predrill tiny holes to prevent the plywood bottom from splitting. Fasten the top to the sides and back in a similar manner.

10. Nail the 17" 1 x 2 to the top and bottom so that the center of the board is 7¼" from the right edge of the top. Make sure the outside edge of the 1 x 2 is flush with the front edges of the top and bottom. This addition not only provides support between the top and bottom, but it also gives support and draft protection between the window and door.

11. Using 1¼" nails, join the window to the top, bottom, right side, and off-center 1 x 2 support. Then attach the door to the window with two hinges. (This is easier if you purchase hinges with removable pins.)

12. Complete the door by attaching a door handle and two eye-hooks, taking care to make a good, snug fit with the eye-hooks. Install weather stripping on the door jamb to improve climate control and security.

13. Attach rubber feet to the bottom of the bungalow so that the weight of the cabinet and its contents will rest evenly.

14. Using clear silicone caulk, fill the inside seams around the floor to help contain any wet matter.

15. Before inviting your snake to move into his new home, allow plenty of time for all of the fumes to dissipate.

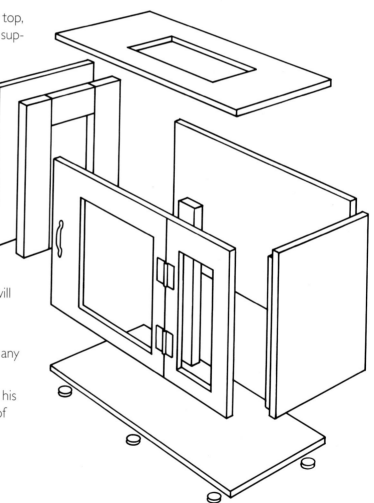

People and Snakes

Throughout history snakes have simultaneously fascinated people and inspired their fear. It was believed in ancient times that snakes never died because of their ability to shed their skin and emerge renewed. That they could move so swiftly and strike and kill large animals, all without the benefit of arms or legs, made snakes seem magical. Many early peoples worshipped serpents, and the ancient Egyptians regarded snakes as the ancestors of their gods.

Not all religious beliefs hold snakes in such high regard. In the Old Testament, it's the serpent that is held accountable for tempting Eve in the Garden of Eden. Greek mythology tells of a gorgon named Medusa, who was a terrible winged monster with a human head and writhing snakes for hair. A single glance into her face would turn a person to stone.

In medicine the regard for snakes has been much more consistent and positive. Early practitioners created potions from serpents' bodies to cure all manner of ills, and today's doctors use the venom from some poisonous snakes to prepare important medications. Snakes have been so highly esteemed among doctors that a pair of serpents intertwined upon a winged staff has become the symbol of the medical profession.

Humans are without a doubt the greatest natural enemy of snakes. Snake meat is considered a delicacy in some countries, and the skins are used to make fashion statements in others. In addition to killing snakes for food or clothing, people have exterminated large numbers of snakes for less honorable purposes. Some areas of the United States hold "rattlesnake roundups," where large numbers of rattlers are thrown together into a pit, then abused or killed in various ways to entertain the on-lookers.

Fortunately, the number of snake admirers is growing. Owning a snake is becoming ever more popular, and reptiles are the fastest growing segment in the pet industry today. As more people come to understand snakes and not to fear them, these graceful animals may finally get the respect they deserve.

Louisa LeMauviel Becker debunks the myth that all girls are afraid of snakes.

Turtle Tub

Design: Ralph Schmitt

If you'd like to have a naturalistic play space for your freshwater turtles in addition to their more practical aquarium set-up, here is a fun project. It takes just a few simple materials to create an environment that includes a swimming hole and some dry ground for basking. Don't forget to place a heat lamp nearby to keep your turtles warm while they play. Here four young turtles—a yellow belly, a map turtle, and two red-eared sliders— enthusiastically explore their surroundings.

INSTRUCTIONS

◆ **1.** Choose a tub or large, deep pan in the size and shape you want for your turtles. Based upon its dimensions, create an armature for making a concrete ramp and pool.

◆ **2.** In this project, the basic shape of the ramp/pool assembly is a crescent. Begin by cutting a 14"-diameter circle of plywood. Using a curve with the same radius as the circle, cut out a portion of the circle to make a crescent (fig. 1).

◆ **3.** Use tin snips to cut a piece of metal lath long enough to wrap all around the perimeter of the plywood crescent. Then fasten the lath to the edges of the plywood with the staple gun, making a wall entirely around the crescent. Where the two ends of the lath meet, join them at the top with a small piece of wire.

◆ **4.** Cut a second piece of lath to use as a ramp leading from the top of the lath wall to the plywood floor (fig. 2). This is easiest if you place the top of the ramp at one corner of the inside curve of the crescent. Cut the ramp long enough so that it provides a gentle slope down to the bottom. Fasten it to the wall at the top with wire and to the plywood at the bottom with staples. Don't worry about neatness; the armature will be completely covered by concrete.

SUGGESTED TOOLS

Jigsaw
Metal snips
Staple gun
Trowel
Large paintbrush (old)

MATERIALS LIST

2' dia. galvanized steel washtub
½" x 14" x 14" plywood
2' x 4' sheet of metal (steel) lath
Fencing material: pieces of
    bamboo, wood lath, or other

HARDWARE & SUPPLIES

Fine-gauge wire
40 lb. bag of vinyl concrete
Latex additive
Curable masonry waterproofing
Red masonry dye
Gravel
Potting soil
Plants
Pea gravel

◆ **5.** Finally, cut a triangular piece of lath to make an inside wall adjacent to the ramp. Attach this with wire.

◆ **6.** Following the manufacturer's instructions, mix a portion of the vinyl concrete with the latex

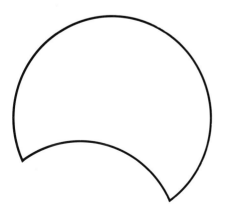

Figure 1

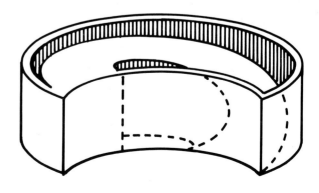

Figure 2

additive. Trowel the concrete onto the armature and use an old brush to even out the thickness and smooth the surface. For best results, work in sections at a time. Start by covering the perimeter wall. After allowing this to dry for a day, cover the interior wall, ramp, and rim of the outside wall. Wait a day. Then turn over the form and apply concrete to the bottom surface.

◆ **7.** After all of the concrete has dried, waterproof every surface. Use a substance designed for curable masonry and color it, if desired, with red masonry dye to give the structure a more natural appearance.

◆ **8.** Allow several days for all the materials to cure completely and for any chemical residue to dissipate. It should have no noticeable odor. Then soak the structure in water for a few days, changing the water periodically, to make sure there are no chemical traces remaining.

◆ **9.** To assemble the environment, place the concrete form into the tub and cover the bottom of the tub around the form with a thick layer of gravel. Add potting soil and plants where desired. A covering of pea gravel over the soil makes an attractive surface and helps keep the pool of water cleaner. (Keep in mind when watering the plants that your only drainage is the gravel at the bottom; don't overwater them.)

◆ **10.** To keep your turtles safe and secure, you must provide a barrier so that they won't crawl out and fall over the edge of the tub. An easy way to handle this is to place the ramp and pool low enough in the tub so that the metal wall of the tub itself is too high for them to scale. You can hide the metal wall with a fence made of bamboo canes as shown here or with a wooden fence of your own design. The bamboo barrier can be made more secure by weaving the stakes together with wire, strong thread, or string.

Turtles, Tortoises & Terrapins

Older than the dinosaurs are the shelled reptiles we call turtles. They first appeared during the latter part of the Paleozoic era, and today there are more than 200 species living in the oceans, on land, and in ponds and rivers throughout most parts of the world.

In casual conversation, all of these reptiles are known as turtles, but in more scientific circles, only the marine creatures are called turtles. Land animals are tortoises, and those dwelling in fresh water are terrapins. All have exterior shells that provide camouflage and protection against predators, and all lay their eggs on land.

One of the most distinguishing features of each animal is its shell, which has adapted in shape and form to suit its surroundings. Tortoises look ungainly because their shells tend to be high-backed or covered with knobby projections. These features make it difficult for predators to get their jaws around the body of the tortoise. The flatter shells of turtles and terrapins are more streamlined to provide less resistance in the water.

Two of the most popular pet turtles are red-eared sliders and box turtles. The red-eared slider is a freshwater terrapin that got its name from the bright red stripe on each side of its head. The box turtle is so called because of its ability to withdraw its legs and head into its shell, then pull up a portion of its lower shell (the plastron) to seal itself into a box. Both creatures are gentle by nature and make delightful pets.

Maintaining a good home for red-eared sliders and other freshwater terrapins is fairly easy. Their basic requirements include an enclosure large enough to accommodate an appropriate amount of water for swimming *and* a dry area accessible to the turtle for basking, a source of heat, and the proper food. Regular care of a turtle and maintenance of his home is crucial. On a daily basis, monitor the health of your turtle by checking his feeding habits, activity level, and overall condition. Plan on changing the water every week because turtles tend to be messy eaters. To maintain the proper water temperature 24 hours a day, invest in an aquarium heater and thermometer.

Box turtles, like all tortoises, live on dry land, and their homes can be made indoors, outdoors, or some combination of both. An outdoor enclosure is preferable, as long as the daytime temperature is in the range of 70° to 85°F and the temperature at night doesn't fall below the 50s. Within the enclosure, provide a shaded area, a shelter from wind and rain, a water dish, and a varied diet of meat and plant matter. Make sure to install a secure top made of hardware cloth to keep dogs and other predators from getting inside; to prevent the turtle from digging his way out, extend the walls of the enclosure about a foot into the ground.

For an indoor habitat, you'll need a large container that can be made waterproof, some potting soil, a shelter just big enough to accommodate the turtle, a heat source for the ground (an electric "rock" is one approach), an overhead heat source, a variety of foods, and fresh water. Box turtles should always have a means to avoid excessive heat, so design the enclosure so that the shelter and a significant area around it are unheated. When assembling the habitat, provide enough soil to allow the turtle to burrow into it.

Before bringing a turtle into your home, thoroughly research its care and diet requirements. Most pet turtles never reach maturity because they're neglected and deprived of the vitamins and minerals they need to prosper. Unlike Mutant Ninjas, real turtles don't eat pizza and can't thrive living in a sewer. Acquiring a turtle means taking on a long-term responsibility. Red-eared sliders can live 25 years or more if well cared for, and box turtles typically live 40 years or longer. Some individual box turtles have been estimated to be over 100 years old.

Photo: Bill Lea

This terrapin makes his home in the headwaters of the Homosassa River in southwest Florida.

Serpent's Mansion

Design: Jeff Kuykendall

Large snakes, such these red-tail boa constrictors, need roomy quarters that are sturdy in construction. Eight-year-old Rocky is the largest of the three; he's nine feet long and weighs in at about 40 pounds. If you feed your reptiles live prey as Jeff does, make sure to include the 1 x 12 barriers at the doorways to keep your snake's dinner from escaping.

INSTRUCTIONS

◇ **1.** For the bottom frame, cut two 72" front and back rails from 1 x 4s and cut two 24" end rails from the 1 x 12. Placing all the boards on edge, use 1¾" screws to fasten them into a frame 25½" x 72". (The 1 x 12s on the ends

prevent live rodents from escaping.) Drill pilot holes before fastening and countersink all the screws.

◇ **2.** Cut a 24" bottom center support from the 1 x 12. Place this piece flat on your work surface in the middle of the frame and fasten it to the front and back rails with 1¾" screws.

◇ **3.** Cut two 72" front and back rails and two 24" end rails from 1 x 4s for the top frame. With all of the boards on edge, construct a second frame as before.

◇ **4.** Cut four 36" corner posts from 1 x 4s. As shown in the exploded view on page 80, attach the corner posts to the ends of the top and bottom frames.

SUGGESTED TOOLS

Circular saw
Electric drill and standard bits
Countersink bit

MATERIALS LIST

(6) 1 x 4 x 12' fine-grained wood
1 x 12 x 8' fine-grained wood
$\frac{1}{4}$" x 36" x 73$\frac{1}{2}$" birch plywood
$\frac{1}{2}$" x 25$\frac{1}{2}$" x 73$\frac{1}{2}$" plywood
30" x 82" vinyl sheet
25$\frac{1}{2}$" x 73$\frac{1}{2}$" piece of $\frac{1}{2}$"-mesh
   hardware cloth
$\frac{1}{2}$" x 29" x 72" sheet of acrylic
   plastic
$\frac{1}{2}$" dia. x 12' quarter-round
   molding
$\frac{1}{2}$" dia. x 8' quarter-round molding

(2) $\frac{1}{2}$" x 1" x 12' flat molding or lath
(2) $\frac{1}{2}$" x 24" x 36" pieces of finish-
   grade plywood
(2) 1$\frac{1}{4}$" dia. x 36" dowels
(2) 1$\frac{1}{4}$" dia. wooden finials with screw
   threads

HARDWARE & SUPPLIES

#8 x 1$\frac{3}{4}$" screws
#8 x 1$\frac{1}{4}$" screws
#6 x $\frac{3}{4}$" screws
$\frac{1}{2}$" staples
$\frac{1}{2}$" fence staples
(2) 2$\frac{1}{2}$" hinges
Stain and sealer of your choice
(4) eye-hooks
(4) heavy-duty casters

5. For the center uprights, cut four 34$\frac{1}{2}$" lengths from 1 x 4s. These rest on the bottom center support and are attached to the front and back rails. Position each pair of uprights about $\frac{1}{2}$" apart and drive 1$\frac{1}{4}$" countersunk screws through the rails and into the uprights. (The $\frac{1}{2}$" space between the uprights allows you to divide your cage into two compartments, if desired, by inserting an acrylic sheet into the slot.)

6. Cut two 24" lengths from 1 x 4s for the top center supports. Align these with the center uprights and fasten them to the ends of the uprights with 1$\frac{3}{4}$" screws. Countersink all screws.

7. From the remaining 1 x 4s, cut four 18$\frac{1}{2}$" door stops. Attach these with 1$\frac{1}{4}$" screws to the end rails, placing the stops flush with the top and bottom edges of the rails. The stops allow both doors to make secure contact all around.

8. Attach the $\frac{1}{4}$" birch plywood to the back of the cage so that the better surface of the wood faces inward, where it will be seen from the front.

9. The floor of the enclosure, a $\frac{1}{2}$" x 25$\frac{1}{2}$" x 73$\frac{1}{2}$" piece of plywood, can be made water resistant using several methods. In the project shown, the plywood is wrapped with a sheet of vinyl. The extra yardage is folded over the edges and fastened to the underside with $\frac{1}{2}$" staples. Another alternative is to use self-adhesive vinyl tiles. Attach the floor—protected side up—to the bottom frame using 1$\frac{1}{4}$" screws. Don't use any glue to adhere the vinyl, since it may be hazardous to your reptiles.

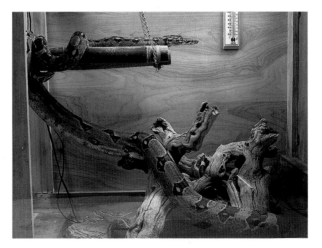

10. Place the acrylic panel on the front, resting it on the front edges of the top and bottom frames. After drilling holes through the plastic, fasten it with ¾" screws to the center uprights.

11. Cut four pieces of quarter-round molding to fit around the outside of the acrylic sheet, mitering the corners if desired. Fasten the molding in place with small screws or finish nails. To secure the acrylic panel from the inside, cut strips of ½" × 1" flat molding to fit all around. Install the flat molding so that it's hidden by the quarter-round molding on the outside (fig. 1).

12. Attach the hardware cloth to the top of the cage using fence staples.

13. On one 36" edge of each plywood door, install two hinges, placing the hinges about 6" from top and bottom. On the other long edge, attach a 36" length of 1¼" dowel.

Then fasten a finial at the top of the dowel. Make sure to drill pilot holes to prevent splitting.

14. Countersink any visible screws and insert wooden plugs. After sanding all rough edges, stain and seal the wood as desired, using nontoxic materials. Allow at least three weeks for all chemical fumes to dissipate before introducing your reptiles to their new home.

15. Attach eye-hooks on each door and place four casters on the bottom.

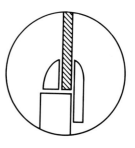

Figure 1

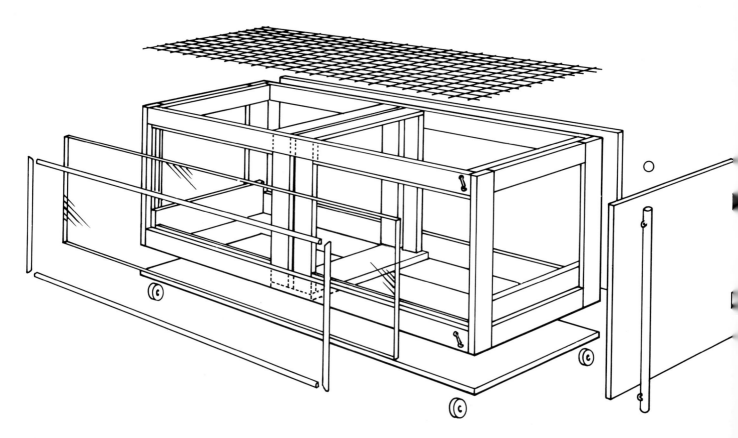

Economical Iguana Cage

Design: Ralph Schmitt

This hanging cage is ideal for a child's room where floor and counter space is at a premium. Just make sure to fasten it to the ceiling very securely, preferably attaching your ceiling hooks to two boards that are screwed into the ceiling joists. This design provides plenty of scope for young and medium-size lizards, such as Beemer, a one-year-old iguana; it's not recommended for full-grown monitors or other heavy reptiles.

INSTRUCTIONS

◇ **1.** Cut a 3' × 6' piece of plywood for the floor of the cage. To reinforce the floor, cut six 2½"-wide strips of plywood, making two strips 24" long and four strips 6' long.

◇ **2.** On the underside of the floor, place two of the 6' strips flat against the plywood and align the outside edges of the strips with the long edges of the floor. Fasten the strips to the floor with ⅞" screws driven through the floor and into the edges of the strips.

◇ **3.** On each end of the underside of the floor, measure and mark 12" in from both long edges. Place the 24" strips between the

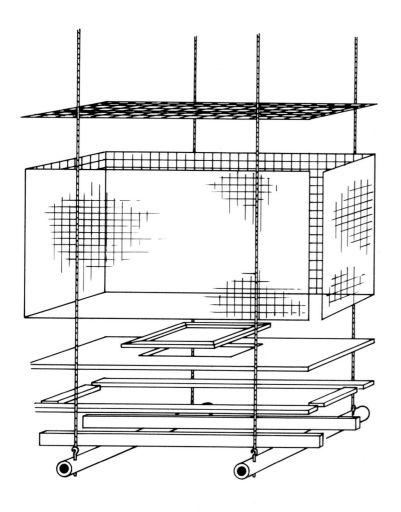

marks, aligning them with the short edges of the floor, and fasten them with screws.

◆ **4.** Place the remaining 6' strips on edge and fasten them to the floor so that they are touching the ends of the 24" strips. Drive $1\frac{1}{4}$" screws through the floor and into the edges of the 6' strips.

◆ **5.** Using a jigsaw, cut a 23" square hole in the center of the floor between the two rails just attached. Since you want to save the piece removed, drill a series of $\frac{1}{16}$" holes to start your cut.

◆ **6.** Cut four more strips of plywood, each $1\frac{1}{2}$" x 24". Miter the corners and make a square frame 24" x 24". Using small screws or finish nails, attach the frame to the square piece cut from the floor. This becomes the door, which can be inserted and removed through the hole simply by holding it at an angle to the opening. Gravity and the oversize frame hold the door in place on the floor.

◆ **7.** Starting in one corner, wrap the hardware cloth around the edges of the floor. Staple the wire to the plywood as you work your way around the perimeter and use your fingers to bend the walls at the corners. When you return to the starting point, cut the hardware cloth so that there are no loose ends of wire. Using the 20-gauge wire, whip-stitch the corner together.

8. Cut a second piece of hardware cloth 3' × 6' for the roof of the cage. Attach it to the walls by whip-stitching the joints with 20-gauge wire.

9. To hang the cage, drill a ¼" hole 1½" in from each end of both pieces of PVC pipe. Insert an eyebolt through each hole and anchor it at the bottom with a hex nut. Attach one end of each trigger snap to an eyebolt and connect the other end to a length of chain. Position the pipes under the floor of the cage so that the door is easily accessible. Install the screw hooks into reinforcing boards on the ceiling and hang the chains from the hooks.

Leapin' Lizards!

With more than 3,000 known species, lizards are the largest group of reptiles. They can be found living on the ground, in trees, and in water on nearly every continent. Lizards differ widely in appearance; some are legless and may easily be mistaken for snakes, and others have elaborate frilly-looking collars of skin that they display when attracting a mate or warding off rivals. Not all lizards are small enough to fit into the palm of your hand; the Komodo dragon, a monitor lizard from Indonesia, can grow to over 10 feet long.

Some lizards, including the larger iguanas and skinks, are mainly vegetarian. Many others, such as monitors, are meat-eating predators that consume insects, small mammmals, and other reptiles. Tree-dwelling chameleons shoot their long, sticky tongues out from their mouths to capture their dinners.

Some of the variation in color and form among lizards is a means of protection. The bright green color of some tree-dwelling lizards enables them to blend invisibly into the surrounding foliage. Others have patterned skin or unusual appendages that match their typical environment. The master of camouflage is the chameleon, which can change its skin color to correspond with the background. Going against the tide is the anole lizard, a type of iguana. An anole changes color according to its mood—it's brown when relaxed and red when excited. A male trying to attract a female performs all manner of colorful gymnastics.

One of the most unusual means of survival common to many lizards is the animal's ability to shed a portion of its tail when it is seized by a predator. The aggressor is left holding a section of tail, which often twitches for several minutes on its own, while the lizard makes its escape. Replacement of the lost section begins right away, and in several months the new tail is nearly as long as the old.

A male anole basking in the sun

Birds

The extent to which man yearns to fly is exemplified in the ancient Greek myth about Icarus, who followed his father up into the sky on wings made of wax, feathers, and thread. In the centuries since, we've applied all our knowledge and technology to the question, and we've continued to fall short. Only our machines can fly; we're still left standing on the ground looking up.

It is our love of flight and our admiration for the creatures that can do it so effortlessly that lie behind our affinity for birds. Then, once in their company, we begin to see more than just their aerodynamic acrobatics. Their jewel-like feathers dazzle us, their lovely songs entrance us, and their personalities beguile us. Birds make wonderful companions, whether you choose a quiet pair of tiny zebra finches or an extroverted Amazon. To share your life with a bird is to spread your mental wings and soar.

Finch House
Design: Ivo Ballentine

Ivo Ballentine is in the salvage business, so it was natural for him to construct a cage from recycled materials when his finches needed a new home. This cage is made with a drawer from an old desk, part of an aluminum window screen, and lots of bits and pieces taken from dilapidated buildings and furniture. The instructions call for commercially available lumber, but your house will have more character if you follow Ivo's example and substitute second-hand materials.

INSTRUCTIONS

◆ **1.** From 1 x 1s, cut four 28" corner uprights, two 36½" bottom rails, a 36½" top back rail, two 20" top end rails, and two 20" center braces.

◆ **2.** From 1 x 2s, cut two 20" bottom end rails, a 36½" top front rail, and two 36½" front spacers.

◆ **3.** Cut two 20" lengths and one 36½" length from the 1 x 6.

◆ **4.** To begin assembling the framework for the back wall, set the 36½" 1 x 6 on edge on the 1 x 1 bottom back rail, aligning the ends. Use 1¼" screws driven through the 1 x 1 and into the edge of the 1 x 6 to join the two pieces along their length.

◆ **5.** Lay the assembly flat on your work surface, with the 1 x 1 member at the bottom. Then lay a corner upright flat on the surface at each end, placing the upright perpendicular to the assembly. The bottom end of each upright should be flush with the bottom edge of the 1 x 1 rail. Fasten the uprights with 1¼" screws, screwing through the upright and into the end of the 1 x 1 and the end of the 1 x 6. Predrill all holes and countersink the screws.

◆ **6.** Place the top back rail between the two uprights and fasten the joints with 1¼" screws. The outer dimensions of the completed back frame should be 38" x 28".

◆ **7.** To construct the front frame, place the 1 x 1 bottom front rail between the remaining corner uprights so that the bottom edge of the rail is flush with the bottom ends of the uprights. Position the 1 x 2 top front rail so that the top edge of that rail is flush with the top ends of the uprights. Fasten all four joints with countersunk 1¼" screws.

◆ **8.** Measure up 3¼" from the top edge of the bottom front rail and mark each corner upright. Then attach one 1 x 2 front spacer on edge (with the 1½" face of the 1 x 2 facing forward) between the uprights so that the bottom edge of the spacer meets the marks. This provides a 3¼" opening for the drawer.

◆ **9.** Measure up 10½" from the top of the spacer just installed and mark each corner upright. Attach the second 1 x 2 front spacer as before so that its bottom edge meets the marks. This should create a 9" opening between the top spacer and the top front rail.

SUGGESTED TOOLS

| Circular saw
| Electric drill and standard bits
| Countersink bit
| Carpenter's square
| Staple gun

MATERIALS LIST

| (5) 1 x 1 x 8' pine
| (2) 1 x 2 x 12' pine
| 1 x 6 x 12' pine
| 1 x 6 x 8' pine
| 1 x 4 x 8' pine
| ¼" x 20½" x 36" plywood
| (2) 1½" knobs
| (1) ½" knob
| (2) 5/16" x ½" x 8' flat molding

(3) ¾" x 12' decorative flat molding
7/16" x 5/8" x 8' flat molding
24" x 13' roll of ½"-mesh hardware cloth
Scrap piece of hardboard

HARDWARE & SUPPLIES

| #6 x 1¼" screws
| #6 x 2¼" screws
| 1" finish nails
| 1½" finish nails
| ¼" staples
| 3/8" staples
| Construction adhesive
| Nontoxic latex primer
| Nontoxic latex paint

10. Lay the two bottom end rails flat on your work surface, placing them parallel and spaced 38" apart, outside edge to outside edge. Set the front and back frames upright at the ends of the end rails so that the outer edges of the corner uprights are flush with the outer edges of the 1 x 2 end rails. After making sure the corners are square, fasten the frames to the rails with countersunk 1¼" screws driven through the 1 x 1s and into the ends of the 1 x 2s. Then attach the 1 x 1 top end rails, making sure all the top edges are flush.

11. Find and mark the inside center points of the front and back bottom rails. Connect one 20" center brace to the rails at the marks.

12. From the inside edge of the left top end rail, measure over 18" and mark the inside surfaces of the top front and back rails. Fasten the other center brace to the front and back rails so that the left edge of the brace meets the marks.

13. Measure the distance between the top center brace and the right top end rail; it should be 17¾". Cut a piece of 1 x 1 to fit and center it within the opening. Join the pieces with countersunk 1¼" screws.

14. To make the drawer, cut two 20½" lengths and one 34½" length from the 1 x 4. Rip each piece to a width of 2¾". Set the boards on edge on a 36" x 20½" piece of ¼" plywood, placing the boards at the perimeter of the plywood so that their outer faces are flush with the edges of the plywood. Fasten the plywood to the boards and join the boards at the corners with 1¼" screws.

15. Cut a 4' length of 1 x 6 and rip it to a width of 4". From this, cut a 38" drawer front. Place the 4" board on the front of the drawer, centering it left to right, so that its

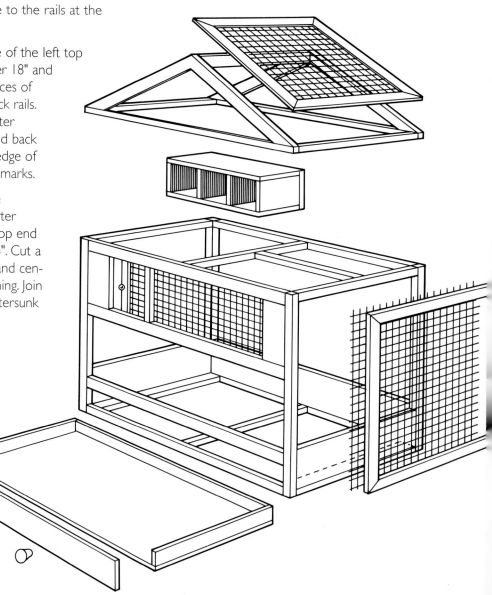

bottom edge overextends the bottom surface of the plywood by ¼". Fasten the drawer front to the ends of the 2¾" boards with countersunk 1¼" screws.

16. Place a 1½" knob 8" in from each end of the drawer front, centering the knobs top to bottom.

17. Cut two 9" pieces from the remaining 4"-wide board to fit into the opening between the top front rail and the top front spacer. Attach one 4" board at each end of the opening, joining it to a corner upright with 1¼" screws and to the top rail and spacer with 2¼" screws. Make sure to predrill the holes and countersink the screws.

18. In the same opening, measure over 6" from the right edge of the 4" board attached at the left end and mark the top rail and spacer. Cut one 9" piece of 1 × 1 and place its left edge at the marks. Connect the 1 × 1 to the rail and spacer after carefully predrilling a hole at each end.

19. To make a nesting box, cut three 18" pieces and four 4" pieces from the 1 × 6. Use two 18" pieces and two 4" pieces to construct a rectangular box 18" long, 5½" high, and 5½" deep. Join the boards at the corners by driving 1¼" screws through the faces of the 18" pieces and into the ends of the 4" pieces. Attach the third 18" piece to the back. Fasten the other two 4" pieces inside the box to create three equal compartments.

20. Place the nesting box in the top left corner of the cage and secure it to the end rail, back rail, and center brace with countersunk 1¼" screws.

21. To build the sliding screen door, cut two 26" pieces and two 10" pieces of ⁵⁄₁₆" × ½" flat molding. Miter both ends of each piece at 45° and join the pieces into a rectangular frame by nailing all four corners with 1" finish nails. Cut a piece of hardware cloth slightly smaller than the outside dimensions of the frame and attach the mesh to the molding with ¼" staples.

22. For the door guides, cut one 18" piece, one 17¾" piece, and one 36½" piece of ⁷⁄₁₆" × ⅝" flat molding. From the scrap hardboard, cut three 1"-wide strips equal in length to the molding pieces just cut. Tack one hardboard strip to one ⅝" face of each piece of molding, placing the bottom edge of the strip flush with the bottom edge of the molding. Use 1" nails driven in just far enough to hold the hardboard against the molding.

23. Inside the cage, place the 36½" door guide against the inside face of the top spacer. The bottom edge of the door guide should be ⅜" up from the bottom edge of the spacer (see the bottom portion of figure 1). Hammer the 1" nails through the guide and into the spacer. Place the door on the guide; then position the 18" guide against the top rail in the 18" space between the top end rail and the top center brace. Allow enough slippage so that the door can slide easily; then nail the guide in place. Finally, attach the remaining door guide to the top rail. On the outside of the door, attach the ½" knob on the left vertical frame of the sliding door.

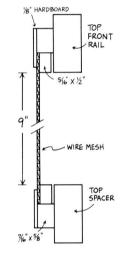

Figure 1

24. For the roof rails, cut two 38" lengths and two 20" lengths from 1 × 1s. Assemble the rails into a 38" × 21½" rectangle and join the corners with 1¼" screws.

25. Cut four 22" pieces from 1 × 2s; then miter one end of each piece at 30° and the other end at 60°. Using two mitered boards, form the front triangular gable and join it to the front roof rail with 1¼" screws driven through the 1 × 1 and into the bottom ends of the 1 × 2s. Repeat with the rear gable. At the peak of each gable, join the mitered ends with construction adhesive.

26. Cut a 20" ridge board from 1 x 2 and fasten it on edge between the gables, joining the ends of the ridge board to the gables with construction adhesive and 1½" finish nails.

27. Fasten the roof to the cage with countersunk 1¼" screws driven through the roof rails and into the top rails of the cage.

28. With the framework complete, prime all surfaces except the insides of the nesting compartments. Then paint the framework with two coats of the desired color.

29. Cut pieces of ½"-mesh hardware cloth to fit the front, sides, and back walls. Cut two triangular pieces and two rectangles for the roof. On all pieces of hardware cloth, allow a ½" overhang all around to provide a means for attaching the mesh to the wood framing. Fasten the pieces using ⅜" staples.

30. Conceal the raw edges of the wire mesh with ¾" decorative molding. Construct a frame for each panel by mitering the ends of the molding and attaching the pieces to the cage with 1" finish nails. For contrast, use ½" molding to frame the mesh-covered opening in front of the sliding door.

31. Prime and paint the molding to match or complement the rest of the cage.

Breeding Finches

One of the most interesting activities to engage in with your pet finches is to watch them breed and raise their young. Once your birds reach sexual maturity—at around 8 to 10 months of age—you can begin making provisions for breeding them. Some finches nest in tree holes and prefer a closed wooden nesting box; others build their nests in dense bushes and tend to favor a small open basket for their nesting site. Allow your birds to make their own choice by hanging one of each in the cage. Then provide plenty of nest-lining materials, such as sterile duck down, dry grasses, moss, coconut or sisal fibers, and soft hay.

Once she begins, the female lays an average of one egg per day and may lay as many as 10 in total. Not all eggs are fertile, and it's common for some not to hatch. During the incubation process, which takes approximately 12 to 16 days, both parents take turns sitting on the eggs. Avoid the temptation to meddle with the eggs yourself, or the birds may abandon them.

While your birds are breeding, they need an especially nutritious diet to restore the energy and minerals depleted by reproduction. Provide them with egg food, game bird starter, meal worms, small insects, sprouted seeds, and other high-protein foods. Make certain they have sufficient calcium and other minerals.

It takes about three weeks for the young birds to begin to leave the nest and another three to four weeks for them to become completely independent. During the weaning process, one or both parents may begin neglecting the young out of a desire to start a new nest. If this happens, simply remove the male and house him out of earshot of the female while she completes her parental chores.

Medieval Tower
Design: Douglas Lapham

From within his tall tower, Edward, an English budgie, delivers a lengthy morning soliloquy in anticipation of receiving his breakfast. The styling of his cage reflects both ancient and modern influences; its overall proportions are mindful of the turrets on medieval castles, but its industrial-style materials are purely contemporary.

SUGGESTED TOOLS

Compass or string, pencil, and
   push pin
Jigsaw
Wire cutters
Pliers
Electric drill and standard bits
Tin snips
Pop riveter or rivet set (optional)
Metal file

MATERIALS LIST

48" x 30" piece of 1/2"-mesh
   hardware cloth
3/4" x 12" x 25" plywood
24" heavy chain
16" x 48" piece of 22-gauge or
   lighter sheet metal (galvanized
   steel, copper, or aluminum)
Interesting branch

HARDWARE & SUPPLIES

Medium-gauge steel wire
2" drywall screws
Short roofing nails
(3) short S-hooks
(3) short medium-strength
   springs
1/8" x 1/8" pop rivets or sheet-
   metal screws
#8 x 3/8" wood screws
Pig rings or heavy-gauge copper
   wire
Small bolt, nut, and washer

INSTRUCTIONS

◇ **1.** Using a compass or a piece of string with a pencil at one end and a push pin at the other, draw one 12"-diameter circle and one 11¾"-diameter circle on the plywood. Then cut both circles with a jigsaw.

◇ **2.** Form the hardware cloth into a 30"-tall cylinder just large enough to fit onto the larger plywood circle (the base). The smaller plywood circle (the ceiling) should just fit inside the cylinder. Allow a small overlap of hardware cloth at the seam; then cut off the excess wire mesh and save it for later. Fasten the seam with short pieces of medium-gauge wire.

◇ **3.** Cut a strip of metal 1½" wide and about 40" long to band the plywood base. The ends of the metal strip should overlap by about ¾" and the extra width forms a lip above the plywood to catch debris from your bird's activities.

◇ **4.** Wrap the metal strip around the base and drill small pilot holes through the metal and into the edge of the plywood. Place the holes ⅜" up from the bottom edge and space them about 2" apart. Then hammer roofing nails through the holes.

◇ **5.** Now mark the locations for two additional holes directly opposite each other (180° apart), placing them near the top edge of the metal strip. After drilling the holes, insert one end of a spring into each hole. On the other end of each spring, insert an S-hook. Then fasten both S-hooks into the hardware cloth to hold the base onto the cage.

◇ **6.** On a large piece of scrap paper or newspaper, draw a 20" diameter circle and cut it out. Fold the circle in half, then in thirds to make six pie-shaped sections. Cut out one section and clip off 1" from the top point. This becomes the pattern for each roof section.

7. Use tin snips to cut five roof pieces from the sheet metal. Overlapping them on the edges, hold the pieces together to form a cone. There should be a large enough hole in the center of the cone to allow the chain to pass through. Using rivets or sheet-metal screws, fasten the pieces together on the overlapping edges. You must drill matching ⅛" holes through both pieces of metal before installing the rivets or screws.

8. Attach the end link of the chain to the center of the plywood ceiling using a small metal strip and two ⅜" wood screws.

9. Before attaching the ceiling to the cage, insert the branch or any other large perches. Then position the ceiling (with chain facing up) in the top of the cage so that its top face is flush with the top edge of the hardware cloth. Fasten the wire mesh to the plywood with roofing nails.

10. Pull the chain up through the hole in the metal roof, position the roof on top of the cage, and drill pilot holes through the sheet metal and into the edge of the plywood. Drill one hole in each roof panel and join the metal to the plywood with drywall screws.

11. From the scrap piece of hardware cloth, cut a door 6" × 6". Then cut a doorway the same size in the wall of the cage. Smooth any sharp edges with a file.

12. Use several pig rings or loose rings fashioned from copper wire as hinges to mount the door onto the wall. For a door latch, attach one end of a spring to the door with a bolt, washer, and nut. Connect an S-hook at the other end of the spring.

13. If decorative trim is desired, cut and fold pieces of sheet metal over the edges of the door opening. These can be crimped or riveted in place.

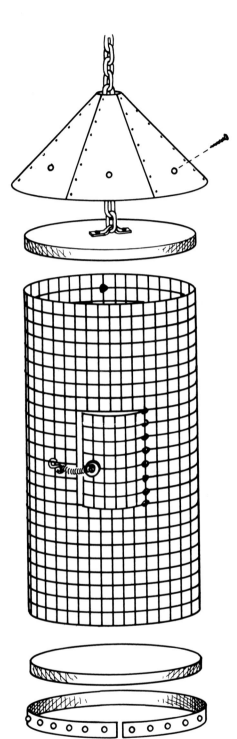

Rustic Perch

Design: Mark Strom

(Mixed-media piece by John Caputo)

Rums, a jendaya conure, finds this rustic perch an inviting place to roost. Equally handsome and functional, it provides a natural setting for any large bird. The top shelf is covered with a thin layer of cat litter to catch any droppings, and the bottom shelf is ideal for displaying house plants.

INSTRUCTIONS

◇ **1.** Select an appropriate branch, keeping in mind that the top shelf must be attached at three points for stability. Separate branches can be used and attached not only to the shelf but also to the pedestal (bottom) portion of the main branch.

◇ **2.** The rectangular base of the perch is a 2 x 4 frame, set on edge. Cut two 15" pieces and

two 32" pieces from the 2 x 4 and miter both ends of each piece at 45°. Assemble the rectangle by gluing the corners and nailing them together with finish nails. Countersink the nails, fill the holes, and sand.

◇ **3.** Cut the 24" x 42" bottom shelf and the 21" x 38" top shelf from ¾" plywood.

◇ **4.** Position the branch on the bottom shelf where desired. Any smaller branches or twigs that overextend the plywood should be pruned. Once you're satisfied with the shape and position, mark the outline of the base of the branch onto the bottom shelf.

5. Determine where you want to cut the branch into the pedestal and perch portions. Keep in mind that there must be three points of contact with the top shelf to hold it steady. To help achieve a flat cut, lay a level across the branch and mark the cutting line completely around the branch. Then cut the branch. Your cuts don't have to be perfect; the top cuts aren't seen and the bottom cut can be adjusted with wedges or by filing.

6. Predrill two or three holes inside the outline where the pedestal will attach to the bottom shelf. Then position the pedestal on the plywood and drill through the existing holes and into the branch. Fasten the branch to the bottom shelf with 1¼" screws.

7. Rip one 1 x 4, making it 1⅜" wide. Cut two 25½" pieces and two 43½" pieces, mitered on both ends, to frame the bottom shelf. Attach the frame so that it's flush with the bottom

edge of the plywood using glue and finish nails. To avoid splitting the plywood, predrill holes slightly smaller than the finish nails. Countersink the nails and sand.

8. Rip the second 1 x 4, making it 1¾" wide. Then cut two 22½" pieces and two 39½" pieces with mitered ends to frame the top shelf. Frame the shelf as before.

9. Position the top shelf onto the pedestal portion of the branch and mark the places where the branch meets the shelf. After drilling a hole in the center of each marked area, replace the shelf onto the pedestal. Then predrill holes into the branch at the appropriate angles. Attach the shelf with screws, countersinking them in place.

10. Place the perch portion of the branch on the top shelf so that it recreates the original natural form of the whole branch. Some additional sawing to level and adjust the branch position may be required; check the position from two views to ensure it's correct. Then fasten the branch to the shelf with countersunk screws.

11. Applying a finish is optional. If you do, be sure to select one that is nontoxic to your bird. The top shelf can be filled with cat litter, shavings, or papers to catch the droppings from your bird.

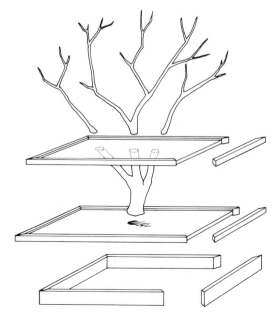

Mild-Mannered Troubadour
or Stand-Up Comedian?

Selecting the right bird isn't quite as easy as deciding upon a new color for your couch. In fact, it's a lot like choosing a mate. Before you allow yourself to become infatuated with the plumage of a scarlet macaw or the trill of a canary, sit down and decide what sort of companion you'd really like to have share your home. Of the two general types of birds kept as pets, songbirds are the relative introverts, and parrots are the show-offs.

Common pet songbirds include canaries, finches, and Pekin robins. These birds are generally peaceful, quiet, and nondestructive; they're neither talkative nor inclined to perform stunts as some parrots do, and most prefer not to be handled. Despite their typically small size, songbirds require fairly large cages that provide them plenty of room to fly. All have very high metabolisms and must have food available in their cages at all times.

There are songbirds for every size family. If you'd like a single bird, choose a canary, which tends to be a loner. Among canaries, males are generally more vocal than females. If you want to have a pair of birds, a male and female Pekin robin or a pair of finches are good choices. Finches are very social birds and can be quite happy grouped in a single cage, as long as the cage is large enough.

There are 300 species of parrot, ranging in size from 5 to 40 inches tall (including tail feathers). The most familiar member of the parrot family is the common parakeet, but the group also includes budgies, cockatiels, cockatoos, conures, lories, and love-birds. As a group, these birds are extremely curious, and they tend to investigate things with their beaks. They can be very destructive, vocal, and bossy. On the other hand, they're quite loyal and exceptionally adept at reading your facial expression and state of mind.

Parrots require much more physical attention than do songbirds. They need lots of exercise every day, and extended confinement upsets them. Parrots that receive insufficient attention tend to bite and display other undesirable behavior, and if they're neglected, they can literally go mad. Acquire a parrot only if you're prepared to make a very long-term commitment; some larger parrots have been known to outlive their human companions.

Minimalist Bird Cage

Design: Ralph Schmitt

If you subscribe to the maxim "less is more" and believe that a cage should be as indistinguishable from its surroundings as possible, then this is the design for you. Its walls and roof are practically invisible, yet they provide a spacious and secure environment for your bird. Snowy, a young cockatiel, has just moved in to this new home and is sampling each vantage point to decide his favorites.

SUGGESTED TOOLS

Wire cutters
Circular saw
Hand saw
Electric drill and standard bits
Wrench
Craft knife

MATERIALS LIST

3' x 17' piece of $\frac{1}{2}$"-mesh
hardware cloth
24" x 36" x $3\frac{1}{2}$" galvanized
sheet metal pan
$\frac{5}{8}$" x 24" x 36" plywood

$1\frac{1}{4}$" dia. x 36" dowel or handrail
1" dia. x 36" dowel
1" dia. x 48" dowel

HARDWARE & SUPPLIES

(2) $\frac{1}{2}$" x 50" threaded rods
(2) $\frac{1}{2}$" couplings
(2) $\frac{1}{2}$" eyebolts
(12) $\frac{1}{2}$" hex nuts
(12) $\frac{1}{2}$" washers
$\frac{1}{4}$" dia. x 48" clear plastic tubing
(4) nylon tie straps
(2) 5" medium-strength springs
12-gauge wire

INSTRUCTIONS

◇ **1.** Obtain a 24" x 36" x $3\frac{1}{2}$" galvanized sheet metal pan from a sheet metal shop or manufacturer of heating ducts. Such pans can be fabricated inexpensively to any size desired for your cage.

◇ **2.** A 10' piece of hardware cloth is required for the sides of the cage, but cut it slightly longer so that you have loose wires on each row on both ends of the piece. Starting with one end in a corner, fit the hardware cloth into the pan, bending it at the other three corners with your hands. When you come to the other end, twist the loose wires together to make a seam.

◇ **3.** Start the roof by making the gables. Cut a piece of hardware cloth two squares longer than 24". Clip the bottom portion of each square in the bottom row to create a row of loose wires to attach the gable to the side wall of the cage. Then, starting at the bottom row of squares and moving upward, successively cut one more square from each end of each row, leaving a single loose wire on both ends of each row, until you create a triangle-shaped piece. The loose wires on the sides will connect the gable to the rest of the roof. Repeat with the second gable.

◇ **4.** Measure the height of the triangular gables to determine the height of the pitched portion of the roof—about 17". Cut a piece of hardware cloth (the full 3' width) that is double that measurement plus two squares. Bend the piece in half lengthwise so that the 3' dimension will match up with the front and rear walls of the cage. To fasten it to the walls, clip the bottom portion of each square in the bottom row on each half of the roof, leaving a row of loose wires on each side to twist the roof and walls together.

◇ **5.** Twisting the loose wires around the adjacent squares, attach the roof to the front and rear walls; then attach the gables at the ends of the roof.

◇ **6.** Measure and mark the center of the 24" edges of the plywood. Then measure in 6" from the center marks and mark the locations for two holes. Drill a $\frac{1}{2}$" hole at each mark to accommodate the threaded rods. Make two holes in the same locations on the metal pan.

◇ **7.** Measure 6" in from the ends of the $1\frac{1}{4}$" dowel or handrail and drill a $\frac{1}{2}$" hole through the dowel at each mark.

8. To include the main perches as you assemble the cage, cut two pieces 12" long and one piece 34" long from the 1" dowel. Drill a ½" hole through the center of the 12" pieces and two holes in the 34" piece, measuring in 5" from each end of the longer piece.

9. Insert the threaded rods through the plywood and into the pan. To hold the pan in place, add a washer and tighten a nut against the pan on each rod. At the desired height, place the lower perch, securing it on the threaded rods with a washer and nut on each side of the dowel. Similarly, place the two upper perches at right angles to the lower one. Complete the assembly at the top with the final hardware and roof dowel.

10. To make a doorway, cut an 11" x 11" square opening in the front wall of the cage. Cut four 11" pieces of plastic tubing and slit each piece down one side with a craft knife. Wrap the tubing over the raw edges of the door opening to protect your hands when you reach in and out of the cage.

11. Cut a second piece of hardware cloth 13" x 13" for the actual door. Hinge it at the bottom using four nylon tie straps, cutting off the excess straps after pulling them tight. Make your own hooks by bending two pieces of 12-gauge wire into finger-sized loops. At one end of each loop, bend the wire into a hook. Make a small loop at the other end to connect to the spring. Assemble the hooks and springs as shown in the photo and connect them to the door.

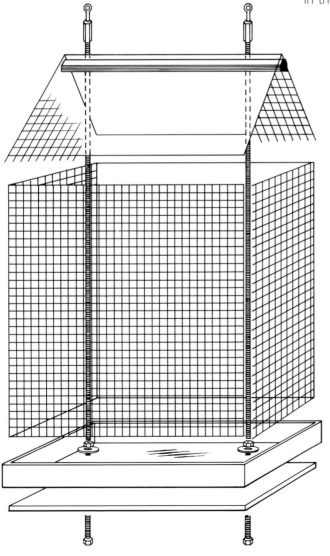

Pie-Wedge Bird Cage

Design: Mark Strom

When Winslow Homer (the cockatiel, not the painter) flew into the yard one day and decided to make himself at home, Mark Strom faced the challenge of adding a new member to an already full household. This efficient design satisfies all of the bird's needs, yet it consumes little floor space. The wedge-shaped cage can be neatly tucked into a corner, and the base is fitted with casters to provide easy access to the door on the back wall of the cage.

INSTRUCTIONS

CAGE

◇ **1.** For the floor and ceiling of the cage, cut two 26" plywood squares. Use a compass or a piece of string with a push pin at one end and a pencil at the other to draw a quarter-circle with a 25" radius on each piece of plywood. Then cut the quarter-circles with a jigsaw.

◇ **2.** Use staples to attach the hardware cloth to the edges of the plywood floor and ceiling, starting at one side of the corner and working around to the other side of the corner. To make this awkward operation easier, work your way around gradually and alternate between floor and ceiling when stapling. It's helpful to have an assistant for this step.

◇ **3.** Use the wire cutters to remove the excess hardware cloth, cutting a straight line through the wire from the top corner to the bottom corner. Measure 16" across one side from the corner and cut from top to bottom. Remove this piece of wire mesh. Insert the two lengths of pipe into the

Figure 1

SUGGESTED TOOLS

Large compass or string, pencil, and
  push pin
Jigsaw
Wire cutter
Circular saw or table saw
Drill and standard bits
Countersink bit
Table saw with dado blade, router
  with straight bit, or hammer and
  chisel
Tin snips

MATERIALS LIST

$\frac{3}{4}$" x 4' x 5' plywood
4' x $7\frac{1}{2}$' piece of $\frac{1}{4}$"-mesh hardware cloth
(2) $\frac{1}{2}$" dia. x $46\frac{5}{8}$" metal pipes
1 x 6 x 12' pine
1 x 4 x 12' pine
1 x 2 x 12' pine

2 x 4 x 10' fir
$\frac{1}{4}$" x $\frac{3}{4}$" x 16' flat molding
$\frac{1}{16}$" x $1\frac{1}{2}$" x $7\frac{1}{2}$' metal strip
$\frac{1}{16}$" x 3" x $7\frac{1}{2}$' metal strip
$\frac{3}{8}$" wood plugs

HARDWARE & SUPPLIES

$\frac{3}{8}$" staples
1" panel nails
#8 x $1\frac{1}{4}$" screws
3" finish nails
#8 x $\frac{5}{8}$" screws
Wood glue
(2) closure hooks
(2) 1" hinges
1" dia. knob
(4) $1\frac{1}{4}$" casters
Sandpaper
Paint
12" lazy Susan (optional)

---

cage and place them in the front corners (fig. 1). Since the pipes are slightly longer than the width of the hardware cloth (to stretch the wire tight), they will need to be hammered into place.

4. To build the door frame, cut two 13" pieces, one from the 1 x 4 and one from the 1 x 6. Rip the 1 x 4 piece to a width of $2\frac{1}{2}$". Then cut two $46\frac{5}{8}$" pieces from the 1 x 4 and rip both to a width of $2\frac{1}{4}$". Assemble the frame by placing the two long pieces parallel to each other and attaching the narrower 13" piece at the top and the wider one at the bottom.

5. Cut two $38\frac{1}{4}$" pieces and two $12\frac{3}{4}$" pieces from the 1 x 2 for the door. Using a table saw, router, or hammer and chisel, cut a lap joint on both ends of each piece (fig. 2). Cut $1\frac{1}{2}$" from each end to a $\frac{3}{8}$" depth for the lap joints.

6. Join the door pieces with glue and counter-sunk $\frac{5}{8}$" screws. Trim the section of wire mesh removed from the cage so that it's $\frac{3}{4}$" larger

all around than the opening and attach it to the door with $\frac{3}{8}$" staples. Cut four pieces of $\frac{3}{4}$" molding to size and use these to cover the edges of the wire, mitering the corners if desired. Attach the molding with 1" panel nails.

7. Mount the hinges $4\frac{1}{2}$" from each end of the door. Position the door inside the frame—adjusting as required—and fasten the hinges to the frame. Install the knob where desired.

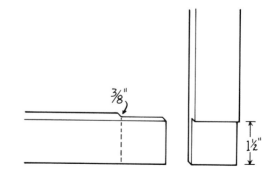

$\frac{3}{8}$"

$1\frac{1}{2}$"

Figure 2

8. Any tree branches or large perches that you want to place inside the cage should be inserted before you attach the door. Then position the door assembly where the hardware cloth was removed, aligning the side edge of the door frame with the corners of the plywood floor and ceiling. Mount the door frame by driving 1¼" screws through the plywood and into the frame.

9. Fasten the cage walls to the door frame with staples. Then cover the sharp edges of the wire with strips of molding cut to length, attaching the molding with 1" panel nails.

10. Starting at one corner and working around, fasten the 1½"-wide metal strip to the top of the cage with panel nails hammered through the metal strip and into the edge of the plywood. Cut off the excess metal at the end with tin snips. Repeat around the bottom with the 3"-wide metal strip.

BASE

11. Cut four 28" legs from the 2 x 4. After sanding, find the center on one end of each leg and drill a ⅜"-diameter hole 1¼" deep to accept a caster.

12. Rip the remainder of the 1 x 6 into two pieces, one 3" wide and the other 2⅜" wide. From the 3"-wide length, cut four pieces, two 20" long and two 18" long. Repeat with the 2⅜"-wide material.

13. Rip the remaining 1 x material into strips 1¼" wide. From these, cut two pieces 20" long and two pieces 18" long.

14. Paint all of the 18" and 20" trim pieces whatever color desired.

15. Assemble one side of the base at a time. Place two legs parallel to each other on your work surface and position the 3" x 20" piece across the top, making right angles with the legs. Align the ends of the trim with the outer edges of the legs and fasten the trim to the legs with countersunk 1¼" screws. Measure 1⅛" down the legs and attach the 1¼" x 20" trim piece using the same method. Then measure ½" down and attach the 2⅜" x 20" piece. Repeat the process with the other two legs and remaining 20" pieces.

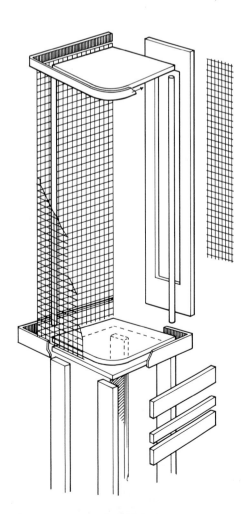

16. To make the other two sides, attach the 18" trim pieces to the leg assemblies in the same sequence, making sure the 18" pieces are aligned properly with the 20" trim to make neat corners.

17. Fill the holes in the trim with ⅜" wood plugs and paint the plugs to match the trim.

18. Cut a 21½" × 18" piece of plywood and fasten it to the top of the base using countersunk 1¼" screws.

19. Screw the cage directly onto the base or, if desired, attach a lazy Susan to make turning the cage even easier. Position the bottom ring of the lazy Susan in the center of the plywood top of the base and attach it with the appropriate screws. Outside the bottom ring but within the diameter of the lazy Susan revolving tray, drill a guide hole through the plywood top. This will enable you to attach the tray to the bottom of the cage.

20. If the tray has no holes for attaching it, predrill three or four ⅜" holes. Place the lazy Susan tray onto its ring; then position the cage on the lazy Susan. One by one, align the holes in the tray with the guide hole and fasten the cage to the lazy Susan with 1¼" screws.

21. Install the casters on the legs.

Eric Lansdown— Michelangelo of Aviaries

San Francisco artist Eric Lansdown is a master of miniatures. His exquisite aviaries are complete in every architectural detail, from terra-cotta tile roofs and elaborate dormer windows to trompe l'oeil stairways and ornamental figures. In style, his designs range from ancient Roman and Egyptian to French Renaissance and Neoclassical.

Although they look like works of art, all of Eric's designs are fully functional as cages for small birds such as finches or canaries. Doors swing open, tops are removable, and bottom trays pull out for cleaning. To avoid harming any potential inhabitants, he uses only nontoxic paints to create the verdigris and other faux finishes that distinguish his works.

photo: Bill Emberly

Ivory Palace, inspired by Britain's Brighton Pavilion

photo: Eric Lansdown

French-inspired aviary on display in the lobby of the Lowe's Coronado Hotel in San Diego

photo: Bill Emberly

Florentine Duomo, created for the AGI-Okinawa Hotel

Small Mammals

Soft, warm, and furry—these are the quiet, gentle creatures that invite your touch. Many will fit easily into your hand or ride comfortably in your pocket. As a group, they're uncomplicated pets, with simple habits and few demands. They make welcome members of most any household.

The smallest of these animals—mice, gerbils, and hamsters—hold an especially strong appeal for children, who can watch for hours as their pets scamper through a toy maze or investigate a new space. Few adults can resist the entertaining antics of an inquisitive ferret or the sweet face of a guinea pig. From the tiniest mouse to the largest rabbit, these animals possess a far greater ability to warm our hearts than their physical size might suggest.

Fairy-Tale Castle

Design: Mary Jane Miller

What could be more fun to watch than two small mice running footloose through a three-story castle? Eleanor and Franklin display the endless curiosity for which mice are known. Up and down the ramps they go, exploring every nook and cranny their play space has to offer. The removable acrylic sheet on the front provides full view of all their antics and gives easy access for cleaning.

INSTRUCTIONS

◆ **1.** Cut four 20" boards from the 1 × 8 to use as the side and back walls of the box. At the bottom of one side wall, cut an arched opening large enough to put your hand through. Save the cutout to use as a door.

◆ **2.** For the base and ceiling boards, rip the 1 × 10 to a width of 8" and cut two 14½" pieces.

◆ **3.** The back and side walls sit on the base to make a 14½" × 8" box. Fasten the 20" side walls to the base by driving 1½" nails through the bottom of the base and into the ends of the walls. Then attach the remaining two 20" walls across the back, fastening them to the base and side walls with 1½" nails.

◆ **4.** Cut one or more openings in the ceiling for air circulation. Then cover the openings with a piece of hardware cloth, securing the wire mesh in place with ½" staples.

◆ **5.** On the ceiling board, measure in ¼" from the front edge of the board and draw a line the full length of the board. Then measure in ¾" from each end and mark those points on the line. Using a jigsaw, cut out a ¼"-wide slot between the two ¾" marks. Nail the ceiling onto the box, placing the slot so that it faces the open front.

◆ **6.** Cut two ⅜" × 20" strips of luan to use as guides for the acrylic sheet. Attach one to the inside surface of each side wall, placing the guide ¼" in from the front edge of the wall. Use ⅝" brads to fasten the guides to the walls.

◆ **7.** Draw the castle facade onto the plywood, using figure 1 and the photo as a guide. The center opening should measure 12½" × 20¾". When you're satisfied with the sketch, cut around the outline with a jigsaw. Then fasten the facade onto the front of the box using 1½" finish nails.

◆ **8.** Using the 1¼" strip ripped from the 1 × 10, cut a piece 12½" long. Attach this piece to the front edge of the base using 1½" finish nails, creating a threshold between the two main towers of the facade.

SUGGESTED TOOLS

Circular saw
Jigsaw
Electric drill and standard bits
Artist's brushes
Tin snips (optional)

MATERIALS LIST

1 × 8 × 8' pine
1 × 10 × 3' pine
Small piece of hardware cloth
¾" × 30" × 30" plywood
¼" × 18" × 24" luan
⅛" × 13⅞" × 22" acrylic sheet
Small sheet of tin (optional)

HARDWARE & SUPPLIES

1½" finish nails
⅝" brads
½" staples
Wood filler
Acrylic paints

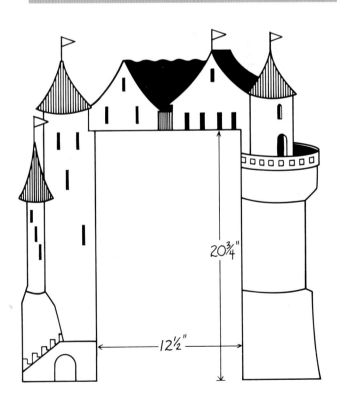

Figure 1

access hole. Then install the floors in the box, securing them in place with finish nails or thin strips of luan placed beneath each floor.

9. From scraps of 1 x material, cut two 3" pieces to use for handles. Center each one near the top edge of a side wall and fasten the handle to the wall with 1½" nails.

10. Paint the castle facade, interior walls, and exterior of the box as desired. Don't forget to paint the arched door on the side to match the surrounding wall, both inside and out.

11. Cut two pieces of luan, each 6½" x 13", for the interior floors. In each floor, cut a 2"

12. Measure the lengths needed and cut two luan ramps leading up to the higher floors. Allow enough length for the top end of each ramp to extend a little beyond the hole in the floor to keep it from slipping and falling out. To secure the bottom end of each ramp, cut a small piece of luan and nail it to the floor for a prop.

13. Slip the acrylic sheet into the slot between the facade and the front of the box to test the fit. The top of the acrylic sheet should extend about an inch above the top of the box. Remove the plastic and drill two 1/16" holes about ½" down from the top, centered about 2" apart. To make a handle, thread a short piece of wire through the holes and twist it into a loop.

14. To complete your castle, fasten the door to the side wall with a small hinge, using a small piece of plywood for a latch. Then cut small flags from a piece of tin and install them where desired on the facade.

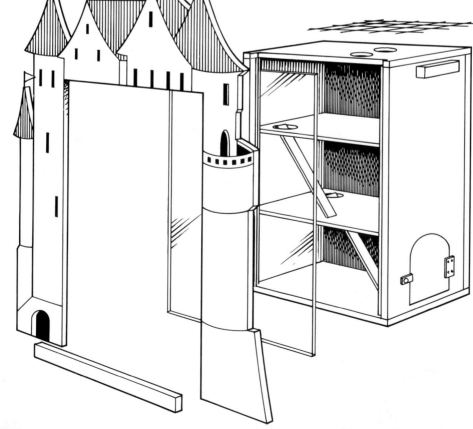

Smallest of the Small

Although all small rodents, such as gerbils, hamsters, mice, and rats, look quite similar and share much in common, each animal has different habits and characteristics. Before bringing a pet into your home, take time to learn which one would fit best with your expectations and your household. A hamster, which is nocturnal, is a fine choice if you're gone all day; if you want to try and teach your pet tricks, choose a rat, which is the smartest of all rodents. Below is a summary of some of the more important qualities of various small rodents; use it as a starting point in your decision process.

GERBILS

Appearance: *Long, furry tail with tufted end; most common color is golden brown with white belly; fur not as fluffy as that of hamsters*

Habits: *Active throughout day and night; very friendly, curious, and hardy; easy to tame; not as nervous as mice; natural burrowers; groom themselves frequently; cleaner than other rodents*

Food: *Plant eaters; commercial pellets are best; fruits, vegetables, nuts, and cheese are good treats; sunflower seeds are highly prized but addictive and may cause obesity; buttercups are poisonous; remove any leftovers daily*

HAMSTERS

Appearance: *Various colors and fur lengths; short, stumpy tails*

Habits: *Instinctively hide food, no matter how much they're fed; easily tamed if acquired young; more inclined to bite than other rodents; nocturnal; can't see well in daylight; need lots of exercise*

Food: *Should have fresh vegetables in addition to pellets; lettuce, fruit, and peanuts are good treats; sunflower seeds are equally desirable to hamsters as to gerbils but just as fattening; remove any spoiled food from hiding places*

MICE

Appearance: *Smallest of all rodents; various solid colors and spotted varieties; long hairless tails*

Habits: *Constantly active; love to explore and hide; very agile; can climb up vertical walls; frequently stand on hind legs to sniff and test environment with whiskers; easily lost and must be watched constantly when out of cage; lick themselves to groom; produce more urine than other rodents, so their cages require more frequent cleaning*

Food: *Prefer cheese or anything else with high fat content; enjoy raw hamburger or chicken; commercial pellets neater and cleaner option; remove any meat before it rots*

RATS

Appearance: *Larger than mice but very similar in appearance; pet rats are smaller than wild ones; pets are white, black, or hooded (black head and stripe down back); long naked tails provide balance on narrow surfaces*

Habits: *Smarter than other rodents; can be trained to come to your whistle or sit and beg for food; more curious and less fearful than other rodents; must be handled daily to remain tame; chewing instinct can be very destructive due to size of teeth*

Food: *Nearly anything; cheese is a favorite; will chew chicken bones and crack open nut shells; green vegetables and some fruits are good snacks*

Ferret Tower

Design: Ralph Schmitt

Buga feels right at home in this multistory play space. The spiral ramp leads from the bottom floor, where she can curl up and sleep or have a snack, to the penthouse pyramid, where she has a bird's-eye view of her surroundings. Access to the litter pan below the cage is through one of the PVC pipes. If your own living space can't accommodate such a large enclosure, simply scale down the materials you use.

SUGGESTED TOOLS

Jigsaw
Electric drill and standard bits
Table saw, circular saw, or hand saw
   and miter box

MATERIALS LIST

2) $\frac{1}{2}$" x 4' x 8' luan plywood
(4) 2 x 4 x 12' fir
(6) 1" dia. x 30" dowels
24" x 50' roll of $\frac{1}{2}$"-mesh hardware
   cloth
(2) $2\frac{1}{4}$" dia. x 5" PVC pipe
Short lengths of 4" dia. PVC pipe
   with elbows and end caps as
   desired (optional)
1" dia. wooden knob

HARDWARE & SUPPLIES

$1\frac{1}{2}$" drywall screws
(2) $\frac{1}{2}$" x 7" bolts
(2) $\frac{1}{2}$" couplings
(2) $\frac{1}{2}$" eyebolts
(4) $\frac{1}{2}$" washers
$1\frac{3}{4}$" finish-head drywall screws
(3) nylon glide tacks
Nontoxic paint or stain
Small wire staples
(4) wire plate holders
(2) medium-strength springs
Round-head wood screw to fit knob
   and $\frac{1}{2}$" washers

INSTRUCTIONS

◆ 1. Cut four 48"-diameter circles from the two sheets of plywood. On two of the circles, draw a spiral with a 4"-wide ramp (fig. 1). The spirals must be identical, and one should be drawn on the smooth side of the plywood and the other on the rough side. (This allows you to keep the smooth side up during assembly, when one spiral is flipped over to become the mirror image of the other.) Drill a $\frac{1}{16}$" hole at the center starting point and cut the first spiral with a jigsaw, stopping the cut as shown in figure 1. Use a nail or other object to score through the cut to mark the other spiral. When both spirals are complete, drill a $\frac{1}{2}$" hole in the very center of each.

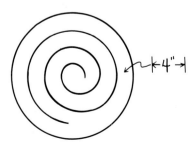

Figure 1

◆ 2. Cut six 23" lengths of 2 x 4 for the vertical supports. On one uncut plywood circle, stand three of the supports on end as shown in the photo (with edges facing out), spacing them evenly around the circle (120° apart). Place each support 1" in from the outside edge of the plywood and attach it with $1\frac{1}{2}$" drywall screws, making sure to drill pilot holes through the plywood first. Repeat with the second plywood circle and 2 x 4s.

◆ 3. Choose one assembly for the bottom section of the cage. If you want to have an outside litter pan, drill a hole in the center of the plywood floor to accommodate a 4" PVC pipe to lead to the pan. This cage has two additional holes and pipes to add interest and give access to other play areas for the ferret. A capped-off length of pipe provides an interesting play space, and the uncapped pipe gives the ferret free rein of the house. The access holes on this project are evenly spaced between the 2 x 4 supports.

◆ 4. In the top section, drill a few 4" holes in the ceiling to provide access to the top floor. Be sure to place the holes well within the triangular area that will be covered by the hardware cloth pyramid (refer to step 10).

5. With the smooth side facing up, place one spiral-cut circle onto the tops of the supports of the bottom section. Attach the outer ring of the spiral to the 2 x 4s with drywall screws. Pull the center of the spiral down to meet the circular bottom floor, mark the floor through the ½" hole in the spiral, and drill a matching ½" hole at the mark. Connect the spiral to the floor as shown in figure 2. Insert a 7" bolt up through the floor, apply a 5" length of 2¼"-diameter PVC pipe as a spacer, pass the bolt through the spiral, add a washer and ½" coupling, and attach an eyebolt. Screw the assembly together tightly.

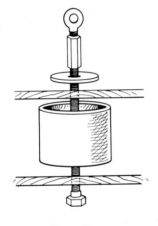

Figure 2

6. With the rough side facing up, place the second spiral onto the tops of the supports of the top section. Attach it as before. When you turn over the top assembly and place it onto the bottom section, you should achieve a continuous two-story spiral.

7. Three dowels anchor each spiral in place. Miter one end of each dowel at 30° and hold it in position against the spiral. The total length needed should be about 27" but measure each dowel to fit exactly. Space the dowels evenly around the plywood circles at midpoints between the 2 x 4 supports. Predrill holes through the plywood at top and bottom and into the ends of the dowels before fastening them together with drywall screws.

8. Pull the edges of the spiral to the dowels, mark, and drill pilot holes through the dowels and into the spiral. Use a bit slightly smaller than the screw and drill a slightly shorter hole. Attach the dowels with 1¾" finish-head drywall screws.

9. To make the legs, construct three 18" equilateral triangles from 2 x 4s, setting the boards on edge to form the triangles. Either miter the corners at 30° or make overlap joints (fig. 3) to form the triangles; then attach the boards together with drywall screws. Trim off the bottom point of each leg to provide enough space to install a nylon glide tack. Attach the tacks onto the legs and fasten the legs to the bottom of the cage.

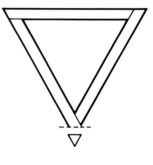

Figure 3

10. For the pyramid at the top, make another equilateral triangle from 2 x 4s, placing the boards on edge. Each side should be about 39" long to fit onto the circle. An option to make a neater fit is to bevel the top edge of each board of the triangle at 30°. Connect the boards with drywall screws.

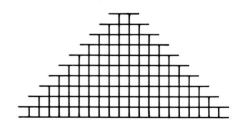

Figure 4

11. Paint or finish the components of the cage as desired, making sure to use nontoxic materials.

12. Cut three pieces of hardware cloth slightly longer than 39". Starting at the bottom row and moving upward, successively cut one more square from each end of each row, leaving a single loose wire on both ends of each row, until you create a triangle-shaped piece (fig. 4). The loose wires will be twisted together with those of the adjacent piece.

13. When all three triangular pieces are complete, staple them to the top edges of the 2 × 4 triangle. Then twist the wires together at the seams to make the sides of the pyramid.

14. Cut two pieces of hardware cloth, each long enough to wrap once around the cage—about 151". Use staples to attach the wire to the plywood at top and bottom on each section of the cage. Where the ends of the hardware cloth meet, twist the loose wires together as before.

15. Cut an opening in the hardware cloth wherever a doorway is desired. For the door itself, cut a piece of hardware cloth slightly larger than the opening. Attach the door to the wall of the cage with two pairs of wire plate holders, each pair connected by a spring. Attach two metal picture hooks on the other side of the door. Complete the door by adding a knob, fastening it in place with two washers and a round-head screw.

16. If you want to keep your cage portable, don't fasten the top and bottom sections together; simply allow the weight of the components to hold the structure in place. Anchor the rooftop pyramid with cleats—blocks of wood—attached to the top of the cage at the corners. Then it's easy to pull off the pyramid when you want to carry each section of the cage through a doorway.

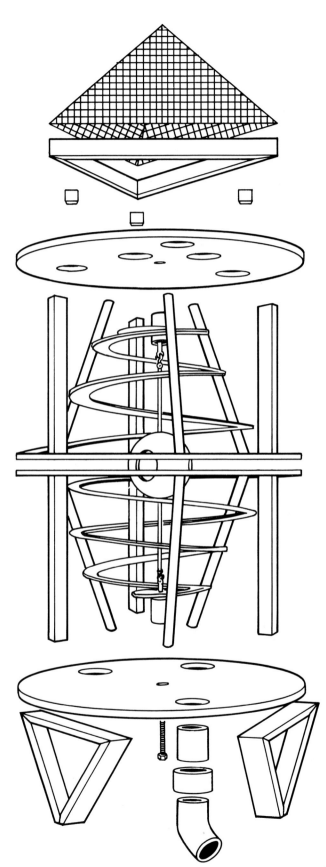

Born to Play

Domestic ferrets are just plain misunderstood. Contrary to popular opinion, ferrets are not wild animals; they were domesticated by humans at least 500 years before cats were. In fact, some cultures considered ferrets to be better mousers and more desirable as pets than cats. Today's pet ferrets are so dependent upon their human connection that they can survive only a few days in the wild on their own.

In many households, ferrets make ideal pets. They combine a dog's sociability with a cat's quiet nature and ease of care. Best of all, ferrets are very clever, and they love to play. They're easily taught to use a litter box, respond to verbal commands, and perform tricks. Not only do ferrets get along well with children, they also mix amicably with the dogs or cats in your family.

Ferrets are naturally clean creatures, with minimal grooming needs. Regular combing helps keep their coats clean and shiny, and they can be bathed using any tearless shampoo. One important area of care is their ears, which should be cleaned periodically with bits of cotton soaked in peroxide.

As with any pet, good nutrition is vital to good health and long life. Commercial ferret food is available from pet supply stores and veterinarians, but high-grade cat food is an acceptable substitute. Dry food is easiest because it can be left out without fear of spoilage. Ferrets tend to eat only when hungry, so they're not as likely as dogs to overindulge. Always have fresh, clean water available for drinking, and never feed your ferret chocolate or other sweets, raw meat, or dairy products.

One of the less desirable qualities of ferrets is their musky odor, and this has probably contributed to the mistaken assumption that they are wild animals. This odor is lessened when the animal is neutered, and it can be further reduced by having your pet's scent glands removed. Proper diet and regular grooming also help.

Unless you want to breed your ferret, you should plan on having it neutered, regardless of its sex. Female ferrets, called jills, come into heat and remain in that state until mating occurs. This prolonged heat leads to two deadly diseases—aplastic anemia and septicemia—which are the two chief causes of death in female ferrets. Male ferrets (hobs) that are unneutered produce a strong, unpleasant odor that is alleviated only by daily bathing. They are also much more aggressive toward other ferrets; during the mating season they may injure or even kill their companions. Veterinarians recommend that all pet ferrets be neutered at the age of seven or eight months, when they've reached maturity.

Buga loves to explore every nook and cranny of her play space.

Gerbil Chateau

Design: Mark Baldwin

With its Mansard roof and clean, simple lines, this country French chateau should appeal to any style-conscious rodent. The solid acrylic floor makes it especially comfortable for gerbils, which have delicate feet that can be irritated by wire screen. A classic front door provides easy access for the animal, but the entire cage can be lifted from its base for easy cleaning.

INSTRUCTIONS

❖ **1.** To make the base, cut two 31" pieces and two 14" pieces from 1 x 1s. Miter both ends of each piece at 45°. After setting your saw to make a ¼"-deep cut, cut a ⅛"-wide groove on the inside (shortest) edge of each piece.

❖ **2.** Assemble the base frame with the acrylic sheet in the groove. Then carefully join the corners with 1¼" nails, making sure the corners remain square.

SUGGESTED TOOLS

Circular saw or table saw
Electric drill and standard bits
Staple gun
Craft knife
Carpenter's square

MATERIALS LIST

(4) 1 x 1 x 8' pine
1 x 2 x 2' pine
$\frac{1}{2}$" x $\frac{3}{4}$" x 12' flat molding
(2) $\frac{1}{2}$" x $\frac{3}{4}$" x 8' beaded molding
$\frac{3}{4}$" x 8' corner molding
1 x 6 x 6" or scrap piece of
$\frac{1}{2}$" plywood
$\frac{1}{4}$" x 3' x 3' plywood
$\frac{1}{4}$" x 12" dowel

$\frac{1}{8}$" x 30" x 13" acrylic sheet
2' x 4' piece of $\frac{1}{2}$"-mesh
hardware cloth
Sheets of coarse sandpaper
Long, thin piece of hobby wood

HARDWARE & SUPPLIES

1$\frac{1}{4}$" finish nails
1" finish nails
Silicone caulk
$\frac{3}{8}$" staples
$\frac{1}{4}$" staples
(2) small decorative hinges
$\frac{1}{2}$" knob
Medium-strength spring
Small S-hook
#6 x 1$\frac{1}{4}$" screws

3. With the base lying flat on your work surface, mark the center points of the two shorter sides and place two evenly spaced marks on each of the two longer sides. At each mark, drill a $\frac{1}{4}$" hole.

4. Cut six pieces, each 1$\frac{1}{4}$" long, from the $\frac{1}{4}$" dowel. Apply silicone caulk to each dowel and hole in the base; then insert the dowels into the holes.

5. From 1 x 1s, cut four 31" pieces, four 12$\frac{1}{2}$" pieces, and four 10" pieces for the cage. If desired, a $\frac{1}{4}$"-deep groove can be cut into each piece to allow the hardware cloth to be inset in the framework rather than stapled to the outside. This makes a neater but less sturdy structure. If you decide to make your cage this way, be sure to orient the grooves properly when assembling the framework.

6. Construct two rectangles for the upper and lower rails. For each rectangle, place two 31" pieces parallel on your work surface, spacing them 12$\frac{1}{2}$" apart. Insert one 12$\frac{1}{2}$" piece at each end to make a 31" x 14" rectangle and join the pieces at the corners with 1$\frac{1}{4}$" nails. Repeat with the second set of rails.

7. Attach the 10" corner uprights to the lower set of rails by nailing through the rails and into the ends of the uprights. Then add the upper set of rails, nailing through them and into the top ends of the uprights.

8. Align the cage with the base and mark the bottom surfaces of the bottom rails with the locations of the pegs. Then drill $\frac{3}{8}$" holes $\frac{1}{2}$" deep into the bottom rails. The slightly larger holes in the bottom of the cage will allow you to lift the cage off the base easily when it's time for cleaning.

9. From the hardware cloth, cut two 30$\frac{1}{2}$" x 11" pieces and two 13$\frac{1}{2}$" x 11" pieces for the walls of the cage. Staple these to the framework using $\frac{3}{8}$" staples.

10. In the lower center of the front wall, cut an opening 5$\frac{1}{2}$" wide and 6" high. Then cut two 7" pieces and two 7$\frac{1}{2}$" pieces of $\frac{3}{4}$" flat molding for the door frame. Miter both ends of each piece at 45° and fasten the pieces together at the corners with 1" nails.

11. The door measures 5$\frac{1}{2}$" x 6" and you can use a piece of 1 x 6 or a piece of $\frac{1}{2}$" plywood. Solid wood is preferable, since the door is well within the gerbil's reach and might be gnawed. (The adhesive in plywood may be harmful to your pet.) Cut the door and attach it to the door frame with two hinges, making sure the door swings easily within the frame.

◇ **12.** Position the door and frame over the opening in the wire mesh and fasten the mesh to the door frame using $\frac{3}{8}$" staples. Complete the door by adding a knob, spring, and S-hook to hold it closed.

◇ **13.** Cut two 31" pieces and two 14" pieces of $\frac{3}{4}$" flat molding to cover the sharp edges of the hardware cloth. With the molding on edge, miter both ends of each piece at 45°. Then attach the molding to the top rails using 1" nails.

◇ **14.** Cut four 31" pieces and four 14" pieces of $\frac{3}{4}$" beaded molding for the bottom edges of the cage and the edges of the base. As before, miter both ends of each piece and fasten the molding to the cage and base with 1" nails.

◇ **15.** To complete the trim, cut four 10" pieces of corner molding and attach these to the corner uprights.

◇ **16.** For the roof, cut two $14\frac{1}{2}$" × 7" pieces, two $31\frac{1}{2}$" × 7" pieces, and one $22\frac{1}{4}$" × $4\frac{3}{4}$" piece of $\frac{1}{4}$" plywood. Then bevel all four edges of the $22\frac{1}{4}$" × $4\frac{3}{4}$" piece at 45°.

◇ **17.** The other four pieces must be cut into trapezoids to create the Mansard roof. On each smaller piece, measure and mark $4\frac{7}{8}$" in from each corner along the $14\frac{1}{2}$" edge. The distance between the two marks is $4\frac{3}{4}$". Draw a line connecting each mark with its nearest bottom corner (fig. 1). Then cut along the lines.

◇ **18.** On each larger piece of plywood, measure and mark $4\frac{5}{8}$" in from each corner along the $31\frac{1}{2}$" edge. The distance between the two marks is $22\frac{1}{4}$". As before, draw lines connecting the marks to the bottom corners and cut.

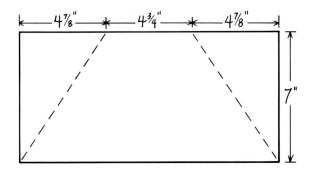

Figure 1

◇ **19.** Position the four plywood trapezoids at the edges of the beveled rectangle. If desired, you can bevel the edges of the trapezoidal pieces so that they fit together more precisely. This isn't necessary because the entire roof will be covered with sandpaper "shingles," and the corner edges will be covered with thin wooden strips as well. Connect the top edges of the trapezoids to the beveled edges of the center rectangle using silicone caulk and 1" finish nails.

◇ **20.** Apply silicone caulk along the side edges of the trapezoids where they meet. To brace the corner joints of the roof, cut four pieces of 1 × 2, each 5" to 6" long. Place each 1 × 2 inside the roof at the upper ends of the joints between trapezoids, securing the roof pieces by nailing through the plywood and into the 1 × 2s.

◇ **21.** Cut 24 strips of sandpaper, each $1\frac{1}{2}$" wide, for the roof shingles. Into each strip, make 1"-long cuts about 1" apart. Begin attaching the shingles with the bottom course, placing the first strip so that its bottom edge overhangs the bottom edge of the roof by about $\frac{1}{4}$". Fasten the sandpaper to the plywood with $\frac{1}{4}$" staples applied along the top edge of the sandpaper. Aligning the top and bottom edges, apply the first course on the other three faces of the roof. Then hold the remaining five strips in the desired locations on one face, with each strip slightly overhanging the one below. (The overhang should be sufficient to cover the staples applied to each preceding row.) Mark the top edge of each strip onto the plywood to assure yourself of even placement. Repeat with the other three roof faces. Then staple the shingles in place, trimming the ends of the strips at the corner edges of the roof

◇ **22.** Cut two 22¼" pieces and two 4¾" pieces from the corner molding. Miter both ends of each piece and join the molding to the top edges of the roof using 1¼" nails.

◇ **23.** Using a craft knife and straightedge, cut thin strips of hobby wood to cover the corner

edges of the roof where the strips of sandpaper meet. Fasten the wood strips to the sandpaper with silicone caulk.

◇ **24.** To attach the roof to the cage, carefully lift the bottom strips of sandpaper shingles and predrill angled holes through the plywood and into the 1 x 1 top rails. Make the holes slightly smaller than the #6 screws; then drive the screws through the plywood and into the rails. The shingles should cover the screw heads.

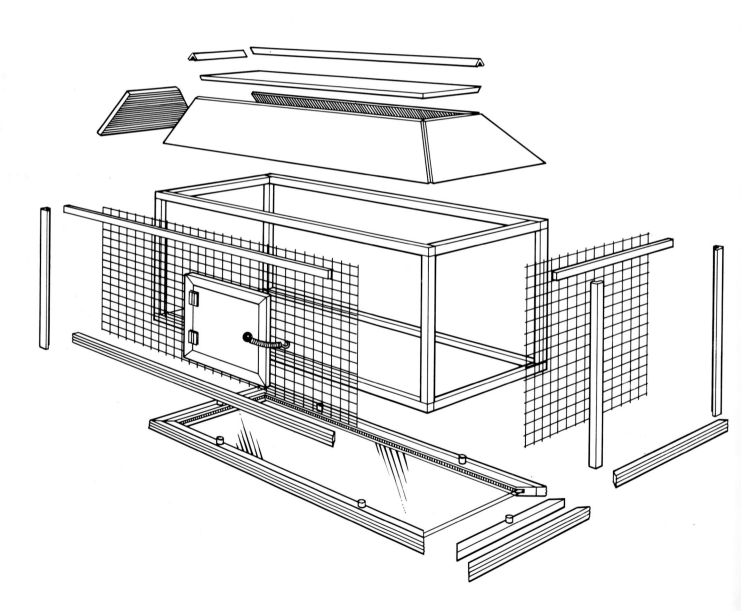

Guinea Pig Barnyard

Design: Reed Todd

Even city dwellers know that pigs and barns go together like oatmeal cookies and a tall glass of milk—one wouldn't be complete without the other. Purrcilla and Sherri are residents of The Health Adventure, a hands-on learning museum in downtown Asheville, North Carolina, where this project was photographed. When given the opportunity to sample this rural alternative, they settled right in and made themselves at home.

INSTRUCTIONS

MAIN STRUCTURE

◇ 1. Guinea pigs, like all rodents, like to chew on everything around them and have been known to eat themselves literally out of house and home. Because of its potential toxicity, no glue is used to construct this project. Silicone caulk, a relatively inert substance, is substituted where an adhesive is required.

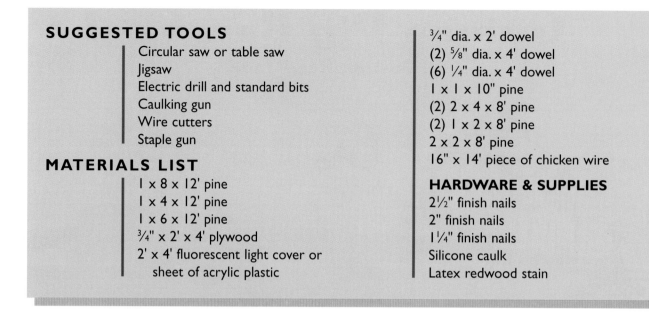

SUGGESTED TOOLS

Circular saw or table saw
Jigsaw
Electric drill and standard bits
Caulking gun
Wire cutters
Staple gun

MATERIALS LIST

1 x 8 x 12' pine
1 x 4 x 12' pine
1 x 6 x 12' pine
$\frac{3}{4}$" x 2' x 4' plywood
2' x 4' fluorescent light cover or
  sheet of acrylic plastic

$\frac{3}{4}$" dia. x 2' dowel
(2) $\frac{5}{8}$" dia. x 4' dowel
(6) $\frac{1}{4}$" dia. x 4' dowel
1 x 1 x 10" pine
(2) 2 x 4 x 8' pine
(2) 1 x 2 x 8' pine
2 x 2 x 8' pine
16" x 14' piece of chicken wire

HARDWARE & SUPPLIES

$2\frac{1}{2}$" finish nails
2" finish nails
$1\frac{1}{4}$" finish nails
Silicone caulk
Latex redwood stain

2. For the first-floor walls of the barn, cut two 13¼" pieces and one 28" piece from the 1 x 8. Draw a doorway in one shorter wall (this project has a star-shaped opening) and cut it out with a jigsaw.

3. Nail the walls together with 2½" nails, making a three-sided box that measures 14" x 28".

4. Make the floor of the second story by cutting one 26½" piece of 1 x 8. Nail the floor to all three inside walls so that the top face of the floor is flush with the top edges of the walls.

5. Cut a 27" piece of 1 x 4 and nail it to the two shorter walls to create a ramp for the guinea pigs to gain access to the second floor. The ramp need not go all the way up to the second floor for the pigs to be able to negotiate it.

6. For the second-floor walls, cut two 14" pieces, one 28" piece, and one 26½" piece from the 1 x 6. Before nailing the walls together, cut openings in all but the 26½" piece for viewing the antics of your pigs while they're inside the barn.

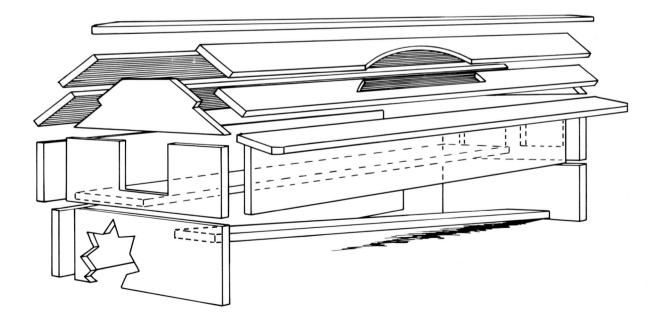

7. Attach each of the two shorter walls to the first story by toenailing 2½" nails into the walls below. Then nail the 26½" wall to the two shorter walls. Reserve the fourth wall until you determine your roofline.

8. Cut two 14" pieces for the third-floor "hayloft" walls. In this project, these walls are cut in a tree shape to create a complex roofline made up of four 1 x 4s and one 1 x 8. The angles can be varied according to your desires; just make sure that the top surface is wide enough for the 1 x 8 and the two steps on each side will accommodate the 1 x 4s. Draw a pattern on one wall and cut it with a jigsaw. Then use the cut piece to mark and cut the other wall. Toenail the third-floor walls in place with 2½" nails.

9. Based upon your chosen roof angle, bevel the top edge of the reserved second-floor wall. Then join it to the two shorter second-floor walls with 2½" nails, nailing through the face of the long wall and into the ends of the shorter walls.

10. To create a stairway for your pigs to go up to the rooftop, stack scraps of wood of various shapes and nail them together with 1¼" nails. Then nail the bottom step to the second floor.

11. Cut four 28" pieces of 1 x 4 for the roof. As before, precut any viewing holes before nailing the roof pieces to the "tree cuts" on the third-floor walls. Here, a 10"-diameter half-circle was drawn onto two adjacent boards and cut with a jigsaw.

12. Cut a 37" length of 1 x 8 for the rooftop. Round the ends, if desired, and cut a 4½" hole placed close to the top of the stairway. Nail the rooftop to the top edges of the third-floor walls.

13. For the overhanging roof across the front of the barn, cut a 28" length of 1 x 6. Angle or round off the outer corners and nail the over- hang to the adjacent roof board and wall.

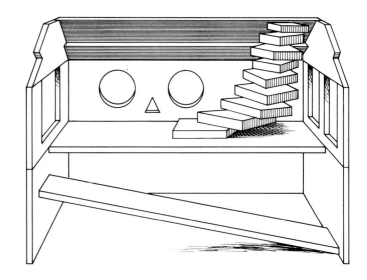

14. Stain the barn, if desired, with latex redwood stain.

FENCED BARNYARD

15. To create the water-resistant floor, first spread caulk on one surface of the 2' x 4' piece of plywood. Then press the 2' x 4' light cover or acrylic sheet on top and allow the caulk to set for at least 24 hours.

16. As shown in figure 1, the fence abuts the barn on two sides and does not continue around the entire perimeter of the floor. Drill ⅝" holes through the plastic-covered plywood for the fence posts and make ¾" holes for the gate posts. Note in figure 1 that the posts are centered 7½" apart, and each is ¾" from an edge of the floor.

17. Cut the two ⅝" dowels into 8" lengths to make the fence posts; you'll need 11 in total. To drill the posts, set them all on your work surface, pressed together between two blocks of wood that are firmly clamped to your table. Align the tops and bottoms of all the posts and use a straightedge to draw a line across the mass of posts 1¼" from the top ends. Then draw a second line 2¼" down from the first; make a third line 2¼" down from the second. Using a ¼" bit, drill a hole through each post at each line.

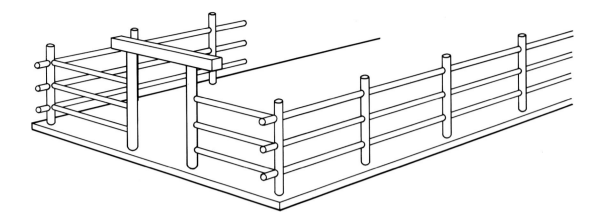

18. Three of the ⅝" posts that you've just drilled will be used as corner posts, and each must have an additional set of three holes drilled at right angles to the first set. Turn three of the posts a quarter-turn and drill a ¼" hole at each line. Make sure not to drill all the way through with the second set of holes; instead, stop drilling when the bit reaches the first set of holes inside the dowel.

19. Cut two 9¾" pieces of the ¾" dowel to use for gate posts. Align the bottoms of the gate posts with the bottoms of the fence posts and mark the gate posts for hole positions. Then drill ¼" holes halfway through the gate posts at the marks.

20. To assemble the fence, start with the longest side. Slip three 48"-long ¼" dowels through the holes in seven of the fence posts, placing one corner post at each end.

Then cut three 19" lengths of ¼" dowel to use as rails for the other long side of the fence. Slip these through three fence posts, placing the third corner post at one end. Cut six pieces from the ¼" dowel, each 7½" long, to use for the side with the entry gate. Insert the six lengths first into the corner posts, then into the gate posts. To complete the fourth side, cut three 8¾" pieces of ¼" dowel and slip them through the remaining fence post and into the third corner post.

21. Test the fence in the holes in the plywood for fit; then apply silicone caulk to the bottom of each post and in each hole. Set the fence into the plywood floor. Once the caulk is completely dry, hammer a 2" finish nail through the edge of the plywood into each dowel to anchor it. Then nail a 10" piece of 1 × 1 on top of the gate posts.

MESH-COVERED EXTERIOR FRAME

22. For the base of the frame, cut two 51½" pieces and two 27½" pieces from the 2 × 4s. Setting all of the boards on edge, fit the two shorter 2 × 4s between the two longer boards to form a rectangle. Make sure that the corners of the rectangular base are square; then join the pieces together by driving 2½" nails through the longer boards and into the ends of the shorter ones.

23. Cut four 18" 2 × 2s for the uprights. Before attaching the 2 × 2s at the corners of the frame, use a circular saw or table saw to

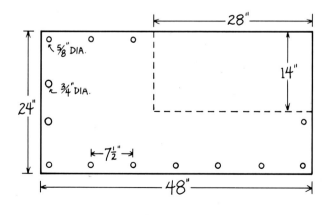

Figure 1

miter one end of each. As you can see from the photo, the miter angles aren't terribly important. Without these miters, however, it would be difficult to staple the mesh at the bottom of the base.

◇ **24.** Using the photo as a guide, place the mitered end of a 2 x 2 at each end of the longer 2 x 4s. Secure the uprights in place with three or four 2½" nails at each joint.

◇ **25.** Cut two 51½" pieces and two 27½" pieces from the 1 x 2s for the upper rails. Fit the upper rails between the uprights, positioning them about ½" below the top end of each upright. Then join the upper corners of the frame by driving 2½" nails through the uprights and into the rails.

◇ **26.** Sand the frame well, especially on inside edges. Then apply latex stain as you did on the barn.

◇ **27.** To complete the structure, wrap chicken wire around the exterior of the frame and staple the mesh to the uprights and the top and bottom frames.

Thanks to the Monks!

Wild rabbits were considered desirable game in countries throughout ancient Europe, and the Romans kept both hares and rabbits for culinary purposes in large enclosures called *lepodaria*. (Hares are closely related to rabbits, but they have longer ears and large hind feet. Further differentiating them is the fact that hares don't share rabbits' instinct to burrow.) These animals were different in appearance from modern domestic rabbits, which derive their variety of colors and markings from the breeding programs of medieval monks.

Early in the Middle Ages, monks began keeping rabbits to feed themselves and the travelers who visited their monasteries. They housed the animals in large hutches and practiced selective breeding among them, which resulted in rabbits with many interesting pelt colors. Wild rabbits are an overall gray-brown, and more conspicuous-looking specimens in nature are relatively short lived. Under the protective care of the monks, however, the recessive genetic traits for color and pattern could be developed to create new rabbit varieties. These hybrids were the ancestors of the domestic rabbits we know today.

Rabbits haven't always been welcome neighbors to humans. The animals were often carried to new lands by early explorers, who took them along as renewable foodstuff. When some inevitably escaped, they often multiplied uncontrollably due to a lack of natural predators. Some such occurrences were known as rabbit plagues because of the degree of damage inflicted by these animals to crops and other vegetation. In Australia during the mid-19th century, conditions were so severe that biological warfare against the rabbits was undertaken.

Marco Polo exhibits some of the beautiful markings common to modern rabbits.

Bunny Haven
Design: Susan Kinney & Ralph Schmitt

Hares and hounds don't mix well together, so the primary role of a rabbit hutch is to provide security for its inhabitants. Marco Polo is a safe distance off the ground in this hutch, and he's protected from cold winter drafts by two solid walls. With its clean, spare lines, this design lends itself nicely to any painted or stained finish you may desire.

SUGGESTED TOOLS

Circular saw or table saw
Electric drill and standard bits
Table saw with dado blade, router
    with straight bit, or hammer and
    chisel (optional)
Jigsaw

MATERIALS LIST

(8) 2 x 2 x 12' cedar or fir
(2) $\frac{1}{2}$" x 4' x 8' plywood
$\frac{1}{2}$" x 18" x 36" plywood
(3) 1 x 2 x 12' fir
3' x 8' piece of chicken wire

2 x 4 x 52" fir or 4" x 48"
    sheet metal for ridge cap

HARDWARE & SUPPLIES

3" galvanized drywall screws
1$\frac{1}{2}$" galvanized screws
1" galvanized screws
1$\frac{1}{2}$" galvanized ring-shank or
    drywall nails
$\frac{3}{8}$" staples
(2) 2$\frac{1}{2}$" hinges with removable pins
Eye-hook
42" screen door brace

INSTRUCTIONS

◆ **1.** Cut four 5' corner posts and four 33" top and bottom rails from the 2 x 2s and use these to construct the front and back frames as shown in figure 1. Join the boards at the corners with 3" screws after drilling pilot holes. For stronger joints, the designer made shallow ($\frac{1}{8}$") dadoes; if you do the same, adjust the measurements in the subsequent steps accordingly.

◆ **2.** Cut four side rails, each 45" long, and attach them to the front and back frames, aligning these with the top and bottom rails (fig. 2).

◆ **3.** For the floor, cut a piece of plywood 3' x 4'; then use a jigsaw to cut 1$\frac{1}{2}$" x 1$\frac{1}{2}$" notches in the corners to accommodate the corner posts. Attach the floor to the bottom rails with 1$\frac{1}{2}$" screws.

◆ **4.** Cut a piece of plywood 36" x 34$\frac{3}{4}$" for the back. The back sits on the floor, just inside the back frame. Cut a 1$\frac{1}{2}$" x $\frac{3}{4}$" notch at each top corner to accommodate the top side rails. Join the plywood back to the back frame with 1$\frac{1}{2}$" screws.

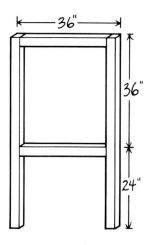

Figure 1

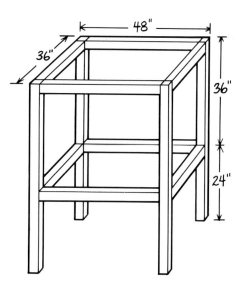

Figure 2

5. Because the back rests *on* the floor, its bottom edge is not attached to anything. Cut a 33" piece of 2 x 2 to use as a brace along the bottom. This brace sits outside the wall, on the bottom rail of the back frame, so bevel the top edge, if desired, to allow rain to run off easily. Then fasten the brace to the bottom rail with 3" screws; use 1½" screws to fasten the plywood back to the brace.

6. Cut a 46" x 35½" piece of plywood for the side wall, making a 1½" x 1½" notch at the top front corner to accommodate the top front rail. Like the back, the side wall sits on the floor, just inside the framework. Attach the wall to the front corner post and top side rail with 1½" screws.

7. As you did for the back, cut a 45" outside brace for the side wall. Fasten the brace to the bottom side rail with 3" screws; then fasten the wall to the brace with 1½" screws.

8. Build the inside shelf by cutting a piece of plywood 18" x 34". Cut one 18" (or shorter if your rabbit is very small) piece of 2 x 2 for a corner leg. Attach the leg to one front corner of the shelf as shown in the photo. Then hold the shelf up to the side and back walls and mark where shelf braces should be attached. Cut lengths of 1 x 2 to fit and attach them to the side and back walls with 1" screws. Attach the shelf to the braces and screw through the floor and into the leg to secure the shelf in place.

9. Establish a roof angle of 30° by cutting two plywood gables as shown in figure 3. Begin by drawing a triangle that is 36" wide at the base and 10⅜" high. Measure over 1½" from each

bottom corner and mark. Draw a ¾" line down from each mark and connect the end points of those two lines. This gives you a triangular gable 11⅛" tall that accommodates the corner posts and provides an extension along its bottom edge that can be fastened to the top rail. Place each gable on the inside surface of the top rail of the front and back frames; then fasten each gable to the frame with 1½" screws.

10. To make the ridge pole, cut a 44" length of 2 x 2 and bevel two adjacent edges at 30° so that the cross section of the board is shaped like a pentagon. Position the ridge pole so that the peak of the pentagon is aligned with the tops of the plywood gables; then fasten the gables to the ridge pole with 1½" screws.

11. Cut two pieces of plywood, each 48" x 22" for the roof panels. Bevel one 48" edge of each piece at 60° so that they meet exactly at the ridge line. Then attach the roof panels to the ridge pole and the top side rails with galvanized ring-shank nails.

12. Cut two mitered trim pieces to complete the framework on each gable. Determine the mitered angles by marking lengths of 2 x 2 with a pencil; then cut them by hand to fit. To attach the trim, apply 1½" screws through the roof panels and into the 2 x 2s. Fasten the gables to the trim for added security.

13. On this project, the ridge cap is a 2 x 4 that has been cut on a table saw set at 30° to remove a wedge-shaped section from the bottom face of the board. Then both top edges are slightly beveled and both ends are cut at an angle for added style. If you don't have a table saw, one alternative is to use asphalt shingles to cover the roof and ridge joint. (See the country cottage, page 45, for instructions.)

14. The door of the hutch consists of a piece of chicken wire held neatly in place by a 2 x 2 outer frame and a 1 x 2 inner frame. This assembly fits within the opening in the front frame of the hutch. To allow for swelling

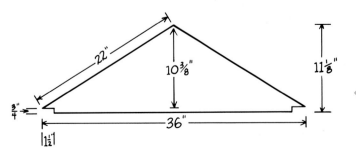

Figure 3

during warm, humid weather, measure and cut the 2 x 2s for the outer frame of the door slightly smaller than the opening. Miter the corners and fasten the 2 x 2s together with 3" screws.

15. Cut mitered 1 x 2s for the inner frame so that they're about ¼" shorter than the inside dimensions of the outer frame. This is to allow room for the chicken wire to go between the two frames. Cut a piece of wire mesh large enough to cover the inner frame and fold over the edges. Test the wire-covered inner frame for fit within the outer frame and make any necessary adjustments. Then fasten the inner frame to the outer frame with 1½" screws.

16. Attach the screen door brace diagonally across the door. This will allow you to adjust the door if it should warp over time.

17. Mount the hinges on the door and hutch frame; then install the eye-hook. If desired, cut a 35½" piece of 2 x 2 to use as a vertical door stop. Fasten the stop to the upper side rail and floor of the hutch just inside the door.

18. Cut a piece of chicken wire 3' x 4' and attach it with staples to the side rails and corner posts on the open side. To cover the raw edges of the wire, cut lengths of 1 x 2 to make a frame. Miter both ends of each piece at 45° and bevel the top edge of the top piece at 30° to accommodate the roof. Use 1½" screws to attach the trim to the side rails and corner posts.

19. To stabilize the legs, cut eight 10" braces from 2 x 2s. Miter both ends of each piece at 45° and attach two braces to each leg. Fasten the other ends of the braces to the adjacent frame members.

Index

Metric Equivalency

Inches	CM	Inches	CM	Inches	CM
1/8	.3	9	22.9	30	76.2
1/4	.6	10	25.4	31	78.7
3/8	1.0	11	27.9	32	81.3
1/2	1.3	12	30.5	33	83.8
5/8	1.6	13	33.0	34	86.4
3/4	1.9	14	35.6	35	88.9
7/8	2.2	15	38.1	36	91.4
1	2.5	16	40.6	37	94.0
1 1/4	3.2	17	43.2	38	96.5
1 1/2	3.8	18	45.7	39	99.1
1 3/4	44.4	19	48.3	40	101.6
2	5.1	20	50.8	41	104.1
2 1/2	6.4	21	53.3	42	106.7
3	7.6	22	55.9	43	109.2
3 1/2	8.9	23	58.4	44	111.8
4	10.2	24	61.0	45	114.3
4 1/2	11.4	25	63.5	46	116.8
5	12.7	26	66.0	47	119.4
6	15.2	27	68.6	48	121.9
7	17.8	28	71.1	49	124.5
8	20.3	29	73.7	50	127.0